INSIGHT POCK

CORSICA

APA PUBLICATIONS
Part of the Langenscheidt Publishing Group

L

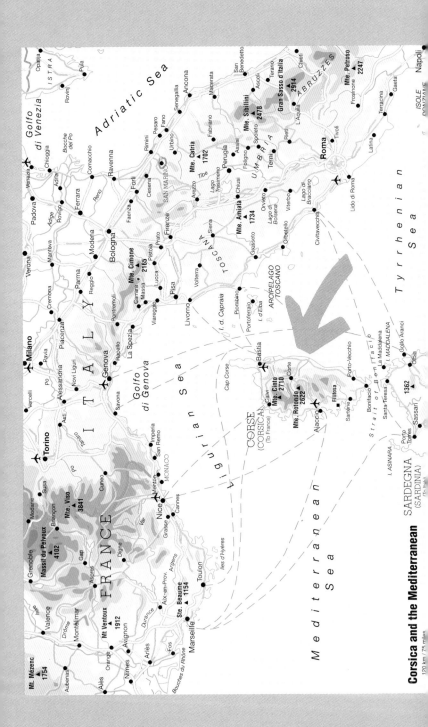

Corsica and the Mediterranean
120 km / 75 miles

Welcome!

Corsica's most famous son, Napoleon, claimed he could recognise Corsica with his eyes closed simply by the scent of its *macchia*, a blend of wild herbs and flowers, on the breeze. Modern-day Corsicans maintain the same, for Corsica remains one of the least spoilt of the Mediterranean islands. Its natural beauty combines with a rich culture rooted in Greek, Byzantine, Italian and French influences.

In these pages Insight Guides' correspondent on Corsica, Alphons Schauseil, brings you the best of the island in 14 day itineraries based around the island's main centres of Bastia, an Italian-flavoured town in the northeast which is well-placed for a tour of Cap Corse; Corte, in the centre (and a springboard for some of Corsica's most interesting mountain villages); Bonifacio, in the south; and Calvi, in the northwest. Each itinerary includes detailed directions for getting around and recommends characteristic restaurants to adjourn to en route. Ideas on where to stay the night are found in the Practical Information section of the guide.

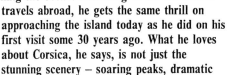

Alphons Schauseil lives in a Corsican mountain village overlooking the ocean. Returning to his home after travels abroad, he gets the same thrill on approaching the island today as he did on his first visit some 30 years ago. What he loves about Corsica, he says, is not just the stunning scenery – soaring peaks, dramatic coastline, and remote mountain villages – but the people, whose very distinct identity he dubs 'Corsitude'.

C O N T E N T S

*Pages 2/3:
mountain
eyrie*

*Pages 8/9:
wind-surfers'
paradise*

Shopping and Dining

Calendar of Events

Practical Information

Maps

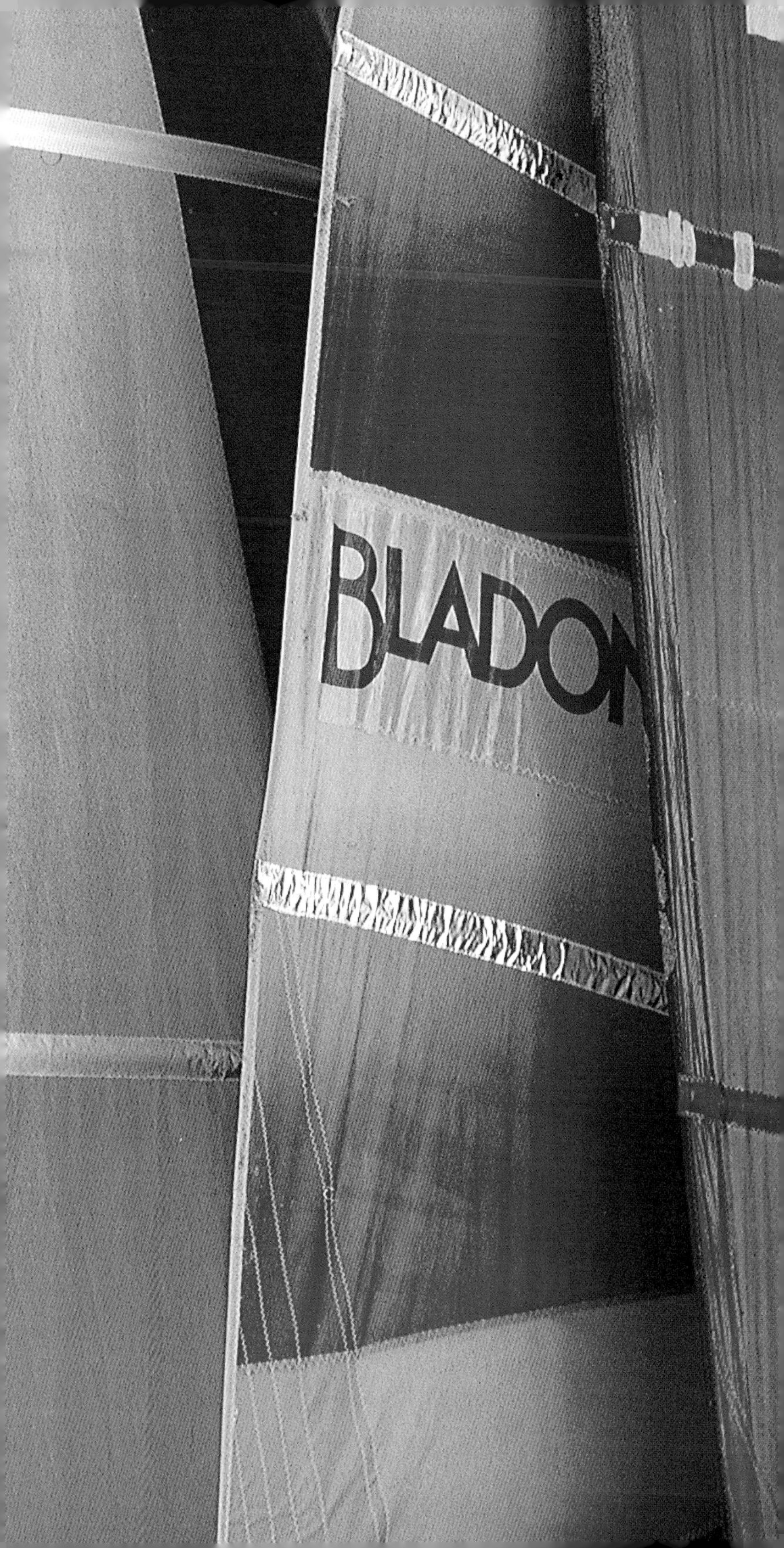
BLADON

HISTORY &

Corsica's first ever tourist arrived by sea 3,300 years ago. The Greek hero Odysseus landed here once the gods had sent him off on his wanderings after the fall of Troy. Homer describes how Odysseus ended up 'in a narrow fjord protected by an unbroken wall of rock' – the harbour in question is thought to be that of Bonifacio. He didn't get much of a welcome: the huge denizens of the island, the Laestrygons, threw huge boulders down on him and his men, forcing them to beat a hasty retreat. These Bronze Age inhabitants do indeed seem to have had almost Cyclopean strength. Their stone forts, mostly round structures called *torre*, were built out of piles of incredibly heavy stone slabs on sites with commanding views. The historians have thus named these people the Torréens.

They weren't the original inhabitants of the island, however.

Vestige of the island's prehistoric past at Fontanaccia

ULTURE

Their predecessors, the Neolithic Corsi, appear to have been peaceful shepherds and hunters. From 4,000BC onwards, though, they seem to have felt themselves increasingly under threat, because they began building *castelli* by adding walls to natural rock formations to make defensive forts. They were also the first people in Western civilisation to create life-sized as well as oversized human sculptures. The Torréens and the Corsi must fused together at some stage to create a people whose actual habitat was the relatively inaccessible mountain regions of the island.

The Romans left their mark as well

Here they retreated to escape the other conquerors who were arriving from across the seas.

Antiquity and Christianity

Around the year 565BC Phocaean Greeks arrived on Corsica, at the mouth of the Tavignanu on the east coast, and founded the trading town of Alalia. They subjugated the Corsicans who lived nearby, forced them to clear the surrounding plains of vegetation, and then had them plant grain, vineyards and olive trees. They also mined ore deposits in the nearby hills, but did not venture any further into the mountains. The Greek historian Diodorus is full of praise for the social system of the Corsi, seeing them as practising 'justice under all conditions of life'.

Greek hegemony lasted for three centuries; after a brief Carthaginian interlude they were finally expelled by the Romans in 259BC. The new conquerors turned Alalia into Aléria and used legion veterans to found a second town, Mariana, on the estuary of the Golu, and several smaller bases all around the island. However, it was only when the Romans' ancient gods were replaced by Christianity that they began to have any influence on the majority of the islanders. A first basilica was built in Mariana towards the end

11

of the 4th century, and the Latin language made its way into even the remotest valleys to become a fundamental element of the Corsican language.

After the collapse of the Roman Empire around AD456, the Vandals repeatedly sacked the island for nearly 80 years until they were finally driven off for good in 534 by the troops of Byzantine Emperor Justinian I. The new lords of the island turned out to be just

as repressive and cruel, however; Pope Gregory the Great was finally forced to intervene in order to keep Christianity on the island. In 774 the King of the Franks and the Lombards, later Emperor Charlemagne, presented the island to the Vatican as a gift.

Ever since the year 700, though, more and more strange sails had been appearing on the horizon. The Moors, or Saracens, of Northern Africa had terrorised the Mediterranean coastline for centuries – and the people of Corsica, bled dry by previous invasions, were scarcely able to put up any resistance. Charlemagne rushed to the island's aid in 806 and at first managed to beat the Moors,

The 9th-century chapel of Santa Reparata

but in the fierce fighting the Corsicans lost 90 percent of their men. However, the Tuscan Count Bonifacio chased the Saracens all the way back to their homeland, and on his return he built a citadel on the southern tip of the island, naming it after himself. But after his death the Moors returned and also set up fortifications, forcing thousands of islanders to flee to Italy.

It was only in 1016 that the Moors were driven off the island by Genoese and Pisan forces. They left a devastated land behind them, and also the anopheles mosquito on the eastern plain, on the Liamone and the Nebbiu.

It wasn't until after World War II that these fertile strips of land were sprayed free of malaria once and for all by the Americans. The Moorish epoch, however, altered the face of Corsica and its traces still remain to this day. The constant threat made the island's population withdraw to the mountains, and right up until recent times they built their villages in relatively inaccessible places, high up in the foothills with commanding views, and always on the lookout for strangers. The coastal strips were nothing more than *piaghja*, or pastureland, to them.

Pisans and Genoese

Settlement along the coast began with the construction of fortified bases by the Genoese and the Pisans between the 13th and 15th centuries. Ever since the defeat of the Moors the two city-republics had been squabbling over the right to administer and exploit the Vatican-owned island. In 1091, a Pope assigned this right to Pisa. Two centuries of peace followed, during which the finest churches on the island were built. The Pisan administrators grew rich and introduced a feudal system, appointing themselves counts and barons. But then Genoa, which had maintained its coastal fortresses, delivered a crushing blow to the fleet of its rival, Pisa, at the Battle of Lepanto in 1284. At a stroke, all the island's riches now belonged to the Genoese.

At first, however, Genoa had to fight things out with the King of Aragon, whom the Vatican had placed in charge of the island. The South Corsican count Vincentellu d'Istria allied himself with the House of Aragon, subjugated almost the entire island with the exception of Bonifacio and Calvi, founded the Citadel of Corte in the island's interior in 1419, and was finally appointed a Viceroy by the Spaniards. He incurred the islanders' wrath, however, when he raised taxes; the Genoese caught him while he was trying to escape and beheaded him.

To defeat the island's feudal lords (*Seigneurs*), Genoa made a pact with the Corsicans in 1359. It assured them protection and a proper system of justice in return for lower taxation. An uprising against the *Seigneurs'* regime led to agricultural reform. North of the central mountain chain, ownership of fertile land was transferred to local parishes. In around 1370 these joined together to form larger units known as *pievi*, governed by *capurali*, whose job it was to represent Corsican interests to the Genoese. As time went on, however, these *capurali* succeeded in promoting themselves to the rank of new lords of the island and ended up embroiled in a power struggle with the *Seigneurs* from the southern part of the island. The ensuing civil war made the island completely ungovernable as far as the Genoese were concerned.

In 1453 the city-republic of Genoa, discouraged, ceded administration of the island to the Genoese private Bank of St George, which was so rich that it could afford its own army. This bank installed a unique early-warning system to thwart attacks on the

Pope Boniface VIII

island by Moorish pirates, which were still posing a problem: they had around 150 towers built along the coast that could provide fire and smoke signals from their battlements. The Corsicans had to do all this work and finance it too, and this also applied to highway and bridge construction. More and more Genoese settlers moved to the island. Despotism became the order of the day, the justice system became utterly corrupt, and mob law claimed thousands of lives. Finally, in 1729, the introduction of a new tax sparked off a general uprising against the Genoese.

The Corsican Fight for Freedom

The Corsican militia finally gained the upper hand. In 1735, a *consulta* proclaimed an island kingdom – but one without a monarch. When, one year later, the Westphalian idealist and adventurer Baron Theodor von Neuhof arrived on the island near Aléria and promised the Corsicans help from abroad, he was instantly proclaimed King Theodore I. The intrigues of the great powers, however, were to prove his undoing. In 1737 a contingent of French troops landed on the island to win back Corsica for Genoa, in return for a large sum of money. The Corsicans were forced to bow to French military might, and their ringleaders went into exile. Until 1753 it remained uncertain who actually controlled the island: France, Genoa or the Corsicans themselves. In 1751, a *consulta* passed the island's own constitution and appointed the worthy General Gaffori as head of government. Genoa cleverly had him murdered.

His successor was Pasquale Paoli, aged just over 30, whose father had also been Regent under Theodore I for a time. The young man, who had studied during his exile in Italy, succeeded in transforming Corsica into a unified state within just a few years. Soon, only the fortified coastal towns still belonged to the Genoese. Paoli created a new justice system that was free of bribery, under which every vendetta killing was severely punished, and this gradually fostered an atmosphere of trust. He divided Corsica up into nine major regions, with Corte as their capital. Under a new constitution, one member of the parliament could be voted for by groups of 1,000 inhabitants respectively, and would then receive one seat and one vote in the *consulta* of Corte. This national parliament was strengthened by a good balance between political and legal responsibility. Paoli actively encouraged education and industry, had some coins minted and created

Pasquale Paoli, Corsica's greatest hero

a national army out of the rural militia. His democratic ideas were a model for the founding fathers of the United States and the ideologues of the French Revolution.

However, absolutism and cold power politics still dominated the mainland. In 1768 Genoa empowered the King of France to win back Corsica and rule there as Regent, and offered him the sum of two million pounds for his pains. Even though Louis XV knew full well that such a sum could never be raised, the invasion began. Early on in the fighting, a French expeditionary force was crushingly defeated by the Corsicans near Borgu, but soon there were more than 30,000 French troops on the island. The decisive battle finally took place in May 1769 on the bridge over the Golo near Ponte Nuevo. The superior force of the enemy finally sealed the fate of the young Corsican nation. Paoli was forced to flee to England.

Napoleon Bonaparte

The French army crushed the last vestiges of resistance with appalling brutality. Members of the nobility who supported France were awarded titles and grants to educate their children at French schools. One cadet favoured in this way was Napoleon Bonaparte, born in the same year the nation was defeated. As Emperor he finally ruled the French and embroiled the whole of Europe in war. But he did very little for his native island.

The outbreak of the French Revolution seemed to provide the Corsicans with one more chance for self-determination. Paoli returned from exile in 1790, and was enthusiastically celebrated as a freedom-fighter even in Paris. But precisely because he tried to keep Corsica out of the confusion and horror of the revolutionary years, the Parisian revolutionaries declared him a traitor to his country. Paoli was forced to flee yet again, and died in exile in London in 1807. The Corsicans made a few more attempts to fight French intrusion, and real calm only descended on the island in 1816. France forgot about Corsica.

Decline and Tourism

As recently as 1911, it was still only possible to reach 300 out of Corsica's 400 or so villages via mule tracks. During World War I, however, the Corsicans suddenly became important. The price they paid was high, though: at least 30,000 men 'fell for France'. The culture that had been built up by several generations gradually became obliterated. During World War II the island was occupied by Fascist Italy, but fighting only actually began in 1943 when German troops withdrew to Corsica from Sardinia. In October that year, Corsica was the first French territory to be liberated. After the war, however, it only seemed possible to make a living either on the Italian mainland or in the colonies. Between 1936 and 1960, the island's population dwindled by half. Whole villages were abandoned.

In 1957 the central government in Paris decided to cultivate the land once again, and to use the island as a source of income from tourism. Settlers – some of them of Corsican origin – returning from the various parts of North Africa that had recently won their independence, created their own monocultures with the aid of state subsidies, and the island's own smallholders had no chance to compete against these newcomers. At the same time, tourist development of the beaches drew the last of the island's young people away from the villages in the interior. This resulted in despair, indignation and finally open protest.

In 1966 the first 'regionalistic' movement was formed, which went on to espouse Paoli's ideas under various different names and became a militant 'nationalism' in the face of unwavering French repression. In 1975 the first violent confrontation occurred. An underground organisation was formed: the FLNC (Corsican National Liberation Front). Using heavily-armed fighters and high explosive, it tried to force the state to accept the idea of a genuine dialogue with regard to the island's interests.

In 1982, after hundreds of violent incidents had taken place, Corsica finally received a special statute and also an island parliament based in Ajaccio. However, the close-knit system of favouritism and nepotism that had established itself amongst all recognised parties during the decades of neglect now led to excessive land speculation for tourism projects, and the underground movement continued to resort to violence to express its disenchantment with developments.

The extended statute that has applied since 1992 still accords the government far fewer rights than those of, say, a federal state in Germany. Despite the fact that some Corsicans have sought violent means to vent their frustrations, the vast majority of the islanders accept and welcome the fact that tourism now plays such an important role in the local economy. The Corsicans are a warm and friendly people and receive their guests with courteous dignity.

High season on the beach at Calvi

Historical Highlights

4,000BC The first *castelli* are built on the island.

1,500BC The Torréens subjugate Southern Corsica.

565BC Greeks from Asia Minor found the city of Alalia on the east coast.

259BC Roman conquests begin.

AD100 Christianity arrives on the island.

456 The Vandals destroy the coastal towns.

534 Byzantine Emperor Justinian I defeats the Vandals.

700 The Moors (Saracens) repeatedly terrorise the island – right into the 15th century.

774 Charlemagne presents Corsica to the Vatican.

1016 The Vatican entrusts Pisa with administration of the island.

1268 The Genoese found Calvi.

1284 Genoa defeats the Pisans.

1297 The Pope makes the King of Aragon new custodian of the island.

1380 The Genoese found Bastia.

1420 Bonifacio, founded in 828 by the Tuscan count of the same name, withstands the King of Aragon's siege.

1440 Genoa founds San Firenze (Saint-Florent).

1453 The city-republic of Genoa cedes administration of the island to the Bank of St George.

1492 Genoa has the citadel built in Ajaccio.

1553 Corsica is occupied by the French for the first time.

1559 The island is returned to Genoa under the terms of the Spanish-French peace treaty of Cateau-Cabresis.

1564 Sampiero, an officer in the service of the Medicis and France, recaptures the island with his men. The Genoese have him killed in an ambush.

1725 Pasquale Paoli born in Merusaglia.

1729 The great revolt against the Genoese finally breaks out.

1731 Intervention of an Austrian army of mercenaries.

1735 A Corsican *consulta* calls for the establishment of an independent monarchy.

1736 Westphalian Baron von Neuhof is crowned King Theodore I.

1738 Second French intervention against Corsica.

1739 Corsica's political and military leaders go into exile.

1755 Pasquale Paoli is appointed national leader in the Castignaccia.

1768 Genoa sells off the island to France.

1769 Defeat of Corsican militia near Ponte Nuevo. Paoli goes into exile in England. Napoleon is born in Ajaccio.

1789 Corsica becomes a part of the French Empire.

1790 Paoli returns from London exile.

1794–6 Corsica ruled by an English viceroy, Gilbert Elliot.

1807 Death of Pasquale Paoli.

1830 First steamship connection between Ajaccio and Bastia.

1914–18 During World War I, 30,000 Corsicans die for France.

1942 Corsica is occupied by Fascist Italy.

1943 Corsica liberated by partisans and regular units.

1955–62 Around 17,500 French colonials from North Africa are presented with land on Corsica.

1975 Two gendarmes are killed during fighting with autonomists. The FNLC underground movement is formed.

1982 Corsica receives a special regional statute without any real rights.

1992 Statute extended with a regional executive. The nationalists receive one-quarter of the vote in the regional elections.

17

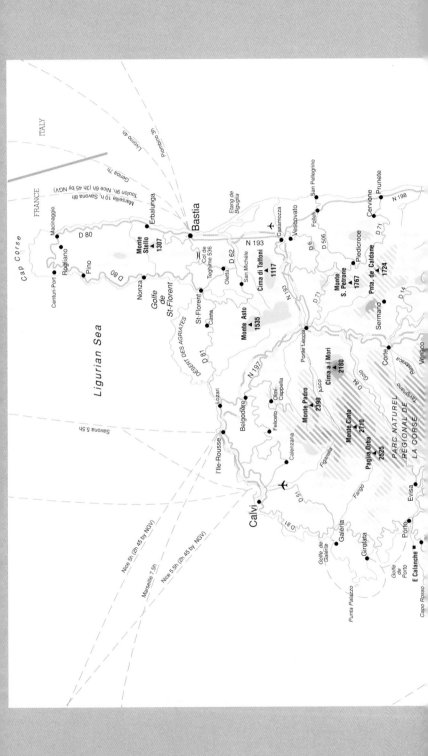

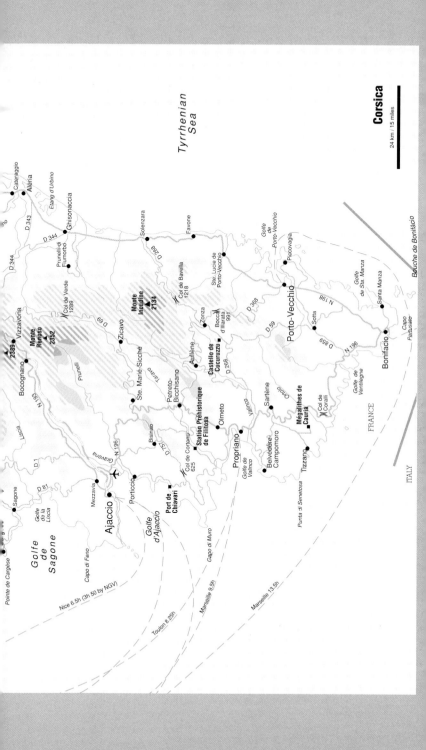

Corsica

24 km / 15 miles

Tyrrhenian Sea

Cateraggio
Aléria
Etang d'Urbino
D 343
Ghisonaccia
D 344
Prunelli-di-Fiumorbo
D 343
Solenzara
D 344
Favone
Col de Verde 1289
Vizzavona
Monte Renoso 2352
2389
Bocognano
Ste. Lucie de Porto-Vecchio
Col de Bavella 1218
Monte Incudine 2134
Zonza
Bocca d'Illarata 991
Zicavo
Ste. Marié-Sicché
Aullène
Castello de Cucuruzzu
Golfe de Porto-Vecchio
Picovagia
Golfe de Sta. Manza
Santa Manza
Capo Pertusato
Porto-Vecchio
D 368
D 59
Sotta
N 198
N 196
Bonifacio
Bouche de Bonifácio
D 859

Liscia
N 193
D 69
Prunelli
Taravo
Petreto-Bicchisano
D 268
Valincu
Castello de Cucuruzzu

Sagone
D 1
D 81
Golfe de la Liscia
Mezzavia
Ajaccio
Porticcio
Bisinao
Col de Cortonu 625
Station Préhistorique de Filitosa
N 196
Olmeto
Propriano
Golfe de Valinco
Sartène
Belvédère-Campomoro
Tizzano
Mégalithes de Cauria
Col de Coralli
Ortolo
Golfe de Ventilegne

Pointe de Cargèse
Golfe de Sagone
Capo di Feno
Golfe d'Ajaccio
Port de Chiavari
Capo di Muro
Punta di Senetosa

Nice 6.5h (3h 50 by NGV)
Toulon 8.25h
Marseille 9.5h
Marseille 13.5h

FRANCE
ITALY

Day Itin

For an island as small as Corsica, the variety of landscape is really quite amazing. Behind the beaches there's a whole hinterland of adventure just waiting to be discovered. Even though I've lived here for so long, Corsica is still full of surprises for me, and I've shared many of them with you in this book in 14 day-trip suggestions based around the island's major centres.

Starting in Bastia, the most down-to-earth of Corsican towns with its distinctive Italian flair, the first trips take you round the **northeast** of the island, including a tour of its 'index finger', the Cap Corse with its quaint fishing villages, the Patrimonio wine-growing district and the fabled Castagniccia region with its ancient hill villages – the very heartland of Corsican tradition.

Then we go up to the island's secret capital of Corte from which you can explore some of the splendid scenery provided by the island's highest **mountains and villages**. The main road down the East Coast brings you to Bonifacio, a town precariously perched on the clifftops and the departure point for a tour of the **south**, first to the medieval town of Sartène and then on to examine some much older vestiges of the island's long and eventful past. Ajaccio is the base for exploring the dramatic **west coast**, including the magnificent rock formations of the Calanche and beautiful coastal villages such as Porto. Calvi in the **northwest** is dominated not only by its Genoese citadel, but also by the impressive hills of the Balagne rising in the background and studded with yet more picturesque villages. For all but the town tours I've assumed that you have your own private transport.

Take the ferry from France or Italy

The Northeast

1. Bastia

Particularly for those who arrive by ferry, a tour of this Italian-flavoured town starting at Place Saint-Nicolas; shops, churches and markets in the Old Town. The port, Citadel and Church of Santa Maria.

Oddly enough, most people who have just been standing at the ship's railing to watch this attractively-situated town approaching, tend to forgo its attractions altogether. Green road signs draw motorists onward like a magnet, either up to Cap Corse or, directly at the harbour exit, straight down into a tunnel leading south-westwards: minutes later, Bastia is far behind.

Napoleon on the Place Saint-Nicolas

But if travelling means absorbing the atmosphere of a foreign place, then Bastia is just the town in which to do it. Drive out of the harbour gates and join the stream of traffic heading for Ajaccio, Calvi and Bonifacio. But when you get to the mini-roundabout with the fountain in the middle, indicate right, and the right-hand lane will lead past a car park. Just before you reach the pedestrian footbridge turn sharp right again – the car park

21

Time for a stroll

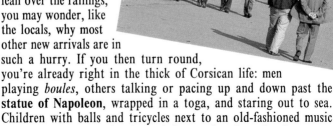

here is also a good place
to leave your vehicle.

A few steps up and
you'll find yourself in
the spacious **Place
Saint-Nicolas**. If you
lean over the railings,
you may wonder, like
the locals, why most
other new arrivals are in
such a hurry. If you then turn round,
you're already right in the thick of Corsican life: men
playing *boules*, others talking or pacing up and down past the
statue of Napoleon, wrapped in a toga, and staring out to sea.
Children with balls and tricycles next to an old-fashioned music
pavilion, *mamans* and *mémés* sitting on benches, chatting away,
and keeping a sharp eye on the young ones. In front of the tall
façades in the background, the wicker-chairs outside the cafés look
inviting: time for your first *café crème* or *pastis*. Bastia is the most
Italian of Corsica's towns. In clear weather the islands of Elba,
Capraia, and Monte Cristo are visible through the trees, and almost seem near enough to touch. In the pavilion housing the Office
Municipal de Tourisme there is a hotel directory, but it contains
no prices. Accommodation for the night can be reserved by telephone
from one of the cafés.

The line of cafés on the square continues on towards the south
and down into the narrow **Rue Napoléon**, where it becomes a

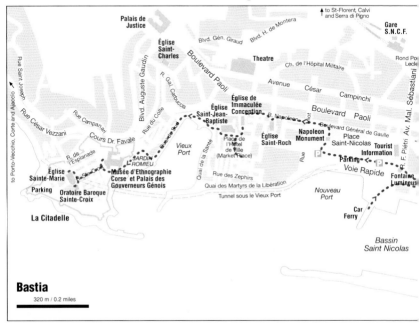

Bastia

320 m / 0.2 miles

colourful mix of boutiques and bakeries, craft shops, and also tiny churches: the **Chapelle Saint-Roch**, the result of a solemn promise made after a plague outbreak in 1598, and the far more magnificent **Chapelle de l'Immaculée Conception** (1704). In front of the latter's portal, colourful stones have been arranged to form a sun, and above the main altar you can admire a painting of the Murillo School. Just behind this chapel a street leads off to the left, down to the morning market in the **Place de l'Hôtel de Ville**. All the smells

and the colours of Corsica are here, and Mediterranean fish glisten in the sunlight in front of the shops on the other side of the square. If you want to photograph anything here, though – even a pile of sausage slices – you need to ask for permission first. Perhaps they still believe in the *malocchju* (Evil Eye)? The first *baguette* you nibble at, or your first piece of *fiadone* should definitely be bought at **Jeanne Galli**, a short distance past the fishmongers on the lefthand side. Almost all the houses in the Old Town are built above fine vaulted cellars like the ones here, and their beauty is only now being rediscovered.

The Vieux Port and Saint-Jean-Baptiste

Go straight back across the market, past the Church of **Saint-Jean-Baptiste** with its very dimly-lit interior, and it's only a few steps down to Bastia's old port, or **Vieux Port**. This is the seed from which the city originally sprang: a strip of sand between the cliffs where the fishermen used to leave their boats. To protect this landing-place the Genoese built a round, massive tower on the rocks opposite in 1380. It was this *bastiglia* (now the *Citadel*) that gave the city its name – older Corsicans still pronounce it *Bashtía* with the stress on the second syllable. An elegant double flight of steps with a small stone landing lead up to the tower. It was later used to form a corner of the governor's palace, which today contains an **ethnographic museum**. Minerals,

The Northeast

Cap Corse

ILE DE LA GIRAGLIA

8 km / 5 miles

- - - Itinerary 2
- - - Itinerary 3
- - - Itinerary 4

Capo Grosso

Barcaggio

Moulin Mattei

Santa Maria

Centuri-Port

Rogliano

Macinaggio

Morsiglia

Capo Corvoli

Meria

Marine de Meria

Couv. de St.-Francois

Meria

Pino

Luri

Punta Minervio

Barrettali

Marine de Porticciolo

Mte. Alticcione

Tour de Losse

1138

Pietracorbara

Canari

1305

Marine de Pietracorbara

Punta di Canelle

Cannelle

Sisco

Marine de Sisco

Marine d'Albo

Guadu Grande

Monte Stello

Genoese Tower

Nonza

1307

Erbalunga

Golfe de St-Florent

Marine de Negru

Sta. Maria di Lota

Lavasina

Punta di a Mortella

Marine de Farinole

S. Martino di-Lota

Miomo

Ste. Lucie

Menhir

Patrimonio

Bastia

St-Florent

Barbaggio

Cath. de Nebbio

D 81

Citadelle

Lavan-daju

Aliso

Col de Teghime 536

Mte. a Torra

Marseille
Toulon Nice

Ligurian Sea

852

Oletta

Sto. Piedro di-Tenda

Col de S. Stefano

DÉFILÉ DE LANCONE

Casatorra

Savona

S. Gavino di-Tenda

Beynco

Borgo

Livorno
Piombino

Solio

Pieve

Murato

San Michele Cima di Taffoni

Etang de Biguglia

1117

Borgo

Mte. Tasso

Lucciana

Plage de Pineto

1372

Campitello

Casamozza

La Canonica

Fouilles de Mariana

N 193

Vescovato
Loretto-di-Casinca

Venzolasca

Ponte Nuovo

D 6

Penta-di-Casinca

Col Saint-Antoine

Silvareccio

D 237

Folelli

Morosaglia

Giocatojo

Piano

Centre de Vacances

Aiti

la Porta

Mte. S. Petrone

Talasani

San Quilico

Campana

Pietra Giusta

Couvent

Moriani-Plage

1767

Coroli

Piedicroce

1183

Valle d'Orezza

San Nicolao

Rusio

Cambia

Carcheto

Carpineto

D 71

Felce

Carticasi

Col d' Arcarotta

Cervione

D 71

Prunete

Punta de Caldana

1724

Bustanico

San Nicolao

Sermano

Mazzola

Pietra di Verde

Chiatra

Alesani

finds from antiquity, old etchings, a tattered flag dating from the last battle against the French... You're sure to understand the island better after a visit here.

The view from the parapet of the Citadel stretches right across the city and its three harbours. The Rue Sainte-Croix leads up to the side facade of the Church of **Santa Maria**, and access to the adjoining Holy Ghost Chapel at the back is through a gateway on the left. The Holy Cross *(Sainte Croix)*, with its figure of Christ carved in ebony, is meant to possess miraculous powers, and according to legend was found floating in the sea by some fishermen in 1428. The church proper, located just around the corner, contains a silver Madonna, Italian paintings and an organ from the Serassi brothers' workshop in Bergamo.

Though strongly influenced by Northern Italy, Bastia is also an accurate reflection of the French lifestyle. The noisy city traffic thunders down the Boulevard Paoli, in which the latest Paris fashions and perfumes contrast sharply with the old narrow alleyways just a few steps away, festooned with washing-lines and so reminiscent of the back streets of Naples.

Most of the city's bistros and restaurants can be found in the streets around the Vieux Port, **Lavezzi** and **Le Romantique** being two very good examples. **La Citadelle** above the port, only a few steps away from the *bastiglia*, is cheap at lunchtime and a real gourmet haven in the evenings.

2. Cap Corse

A trip around the Cap Corse is just **123km/76 miles** long (starting and finishing in Bastia), but it takes a whole day. Magnificent views, watch-towers, a black beach and the finest harbour on the island are just a few of the attractions along the way.

To avoid being dazzled by either the morning or afternoon sun, I strongly recommend that you do the trip around the Cap Corse in a clockwise direction, starting on the west coast. To get there from Bastia, pick up the signs to Saint-Florent at the square in front of the Palais de Justice. The D81 snakes up past the Monastery of Saint-Antoine, and quickly reaches the top of the **Col de Teghime** (536m/1,760ft), which provides stunning views of both coasts. The pass is marked by a German army anti-tank gun; a plaque here commemorates the fact that this vantage-point was taken by French-Moroccan units in October 1943, when the German troops were being shipped across from Bastia to Northern Italy.

The road winds its way down towards the west coast of Cap Corse through the little villages that form part of the **Patrimonio** wine-growing region (*see Itinerary 3*). Just after the village of Patrimonio, take the D80, which you'll be following for the rest of the day, off to the right. It meets the coast at **Marine de Farinole**, and a short distance to the north the hairpin bend at **Marina di Negru** provides another magnificent view, this time southwards across the Golfe de Saint-Florent and all the way to Monte Cinto.

Nonza appears just after you've passed a funeral chapel. Its houses lie huddled against the slope. Above them you can see the square Genoese tower – once the scene of a heroic achievement. In the year 1768, a disabled lieutenant called **Casella** held this tower against a force of 1,200 French troops, using a combination of courage and wit. His fellow-soldiers had deserted him, but he placed their guns in the gaps along the battlements and then fired them one after the other, shouting commands all the while. Once all his powder was used up, he came out on crutches – alone.

An unexpected sight awaits you at the other end of the village. Lean out over the parapet next to the church; below, you will see a good 3km (2 miles) of greyish-black beach, turning even the sea

The view from Nonza

beyond the white line of foam a strange colour – a mixture of turquoise and violet. Tourists like to produce large works of art or spell their names on the beach here using light-coloured pebbles. A path leads down through some overgrown gardens, and past a double fountain called the **Fontaine Sainte-Julie**. St Julie wasn't martyred here in Nonza, though, but in Carthage in the year 303, where she had both her breasts cut off. Here, symbolically, water spouts out on either side of an altar and irrigates a terraced garden.

To reach the tower you have to cross the small square opposite the church. To the south there is a fine view of the pastel-coloured mosaic formed by the various slate roofs, and also northwards straight down to the beach, through a well-placed hole in the rock. At its very end, in **Albo**, the road around the Cap goes right past the colourful pebbles and a fine tower. Swimming here when the waves are high is quite dangerous because of the strong undertow. The small Hotel Morganti retains its old-fashioned charm, in the face of the more modern buildings around it, in its own inimitable way: the sign says that its phone-number is 4 – even though that number has been preceded by nine others for years now.

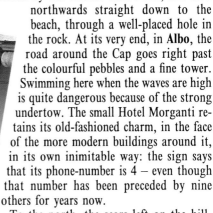

Exchanging pleasantries in Nonza

To the north, the scars left on the hillside by the abandoned asbestos mine are not a pretty sight. If you take the road up towards **Canari**, however, the white bell-tower with its clock, 300m (1,000ft) above the sea, looks quite striking. A little further up there's a portly-looking Pisan church, and downhill the D33 travels past the baroque church of **Saint-François**. A gravestone in front of the altar shows the touching figure of Vittoria de Gentile, holding her swaddled child.

Barrettali is also high up, and near Mineviu there are some magnificent mausoleums right next to the road. From **Morsiglia**, take the road down to **Centuri Port**, which I consider to be the most picturesque harbour on the island. Blue-and-white fishing boats, nets, rigging in all colours of the rainbow, and terraces all around on which the day's catch gets placed. The speciality along this rocky coastline is crayfish. With the sights and the food here, two or three hours pass by in a flash. You're not pressed for time, though: it's only 58km (36 miles) around the tip of the Cap to Bastia.

The round towers in the area had windmill-sails in the old days, and the **Moulin Mattei** with its red canvas roof is just the place for an apéritif. This village is where we say a final farewell to the

Erbalunga

western side of the Cap Corse. If you turn around you'll find yourself looking down at the Corsican equivalent of Land's End, and at the island of **Giraglia** with its massive **lighthouse.** From Ersa, two roads lead to Tollare and Barcaggio on a round trip covering 16km (10 miles). From the 12th to the 16th century the Da Mare family, the Tuscan rulers of this area, used to live in **Rogliano.** Their ruined castles, churches and ornate tombs all testify to the incredible power they once wielded. In clear weather it is possible to see the Italian coastline from here. In **Macinaggio**, Paoli's former naval base, Italian yachts can be seen jostling one another in the harbour.

From now on the road is wider and driving is easier. You pass a few small beaches, the surprisingly well-preserved **Tower of Losse**, and finally **Erbalunga** – almost forming a counterpart to Centuri Port with its ultra-narrow streets, intimate piazzas and its tower. The restaurant with its balcony above the harbour basin is called, naturally enough, **Le Pirate**. **Lavasina** is a place of pilgrimage; the 16th-century Madonna above the marble altar has been ascribed to the **Perugino** school. Tucked away below the coast road are several villas – you're already back in the outskirts of Bastia.

3. The Conca d'Oru

From Bastia to Conca d'Oru, the 'Golden Conch', the former bread-basket of Corsica above the Golfe de Saint-Florent. See map on page 24.

Follow the N193 out of Bastia in the direction of Ajaccio and Calvi. Around 9km (5½ miles) further along this expressway, a sign on the fourth roundabout points off to the right, into the **Défilé de Lancone**, a ravine created by the inconspicuous little Bevinco River. The short winding route emerges at the **Col de San Stefano**, and one of the five routes that meet up here, the D5, leads off to the left, to **Murato**. Just a few minutes later, up on a meadowy slope, stands the Pisan-Romanesque Church of **San Michele**, undisputedly the finest church on Corsica. Its anonymous builders used a combination of green stone from the Bevinco valley and white, yellow and even reddish masonry to create a superb harmony that seems almost accidental. This church, 20 paces long and eight paces wide, has some magnificent ornaments, symbols and naive figures on its facade, and below the slate roof of the apse there is also another re-

The church of San Michele

Fish are landed at Saint-Florent

lief frieze visible, dating from an earlier chapel. The bell-tower, placed on pillars in front of the portal, is unique on the island. The interior contains frescoes as well as carved reliefs from the previous structure on the site, dating from the 10th century. The keys to the church can be collected from the first house on the right along the D162 in the direction of Pieve.

A very different artistic experience awaits you in the former **monastery church** in the village itself. Behind the portal on the right, the *condottiere* Romano Murato had himself included in a picture of Mary Magdalene which he commissioned from Titian or one of his pupils. If the church is closed, just ask who has the key at the Le Monastère restaurant next door; otherwise try at the Town Hall. After this you need to make up your mind: you can either drive through a handful of sleepy villages under dripping cliff-faces around the fertile valley basin of the **Conca d'Oru** and take the extremely sinuous D62 towards the sea, or you can head back towards Saint-Florent along a somewhat faster route. For the latter, drive back to the Col San Stefano and from there to **Oletta**. This town, which was once the capital of Corsica's former wheat-growing region, still has the reputation of baking excellent bread. The D82 leads straight to the **Golfe de Saint-Florent** from here. Roughly halfway along the route you should turn off left and take a look at the **Poterie d'Oletta**, with its superb traditional ceramics.

You should reach Saint-Florent just before noon. There's a large car park on the left when you reach the harbour. If you take a stroll through the narrow streets to the right of the Hôtel de l'Europe and to the square where they play *boules*, you'll come across a shop selling jewellery made of Corsican coral. There are pleasant restaurants next to the water's edge. The little sandy beach opposite can be reached

The limestone Menhir Nativo

from the end of the Oletta road by turning sharp right after the bridge.

On the right, behind the Bar du Passage at the flower-bed with the war memorial, a narrow street leads to the nearby **Santa Maria Assunta**, the Pisan cathedral of the Nebbio. Nebbio (Nebbiu) means fog, and the town that once bore the name, infested with malaria and destroyed by the Moors, was eventually abandoned completely in the 13th century. A glass shrine inside the church contains the mummified remains of the martyr and patron saint **Saint Flor**, presented to the church by the Vatican in 1771. The key to the church can be obtained from the Office de Tourisme in the modern administration building on the left as you leave the town towards Bastia.

Bastia is actually only 23km (14 miles) away, via the **Col de Teghime**, so you can take your time in the wine-growing area of **Patrimonio**. Almost all the growers here will invite you to a free *dégustation* so that you can test their reds, whites and rosés. In the village, to the left of the impressive church, a sign points the way to the **Menhir Nativo**. This is the only known menhir statue on the island that is made of limestone, and it was discovered as recently as 1964 when a vineyard was being ploughed in a hamlet called Barbaggio further up the hill. The roughly 3,000-year-old sculpture now stands to the left of the village war memorial, under a little roof to protect it from the weather.

4. The Castagniccia

The mountains of the Castagniccia dominate the northeastern plain. The region gets its name from the ancient chestnut trees that grow here. Lunch in A Porta, with the possibility of a swim at Moriani Plage before returning to Bastia. See map on page 24.

Passing beneath the Vieux Port, follow the N193 out of Bastia heading south, past the town's ugly industrial suburbs. After about

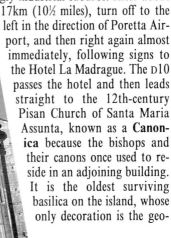

a Canonica

17km (10½ miles), turn off to the left in the direction of Poretta Airport, and then right again almost immediately, following signs to the Hotel La Madrague. The D10 passes the hotel and then leads straight to the 12th-century Pisan Church of Santa Maria Assunta, known as a **Canonica** because the bishops and their canons once used to reside in an adjoining building. It is the oldest surviving basilica on the island, whose only decoration is the geo-

29

metric pattern carved into the southern facade. A few of the foundation walls nearby attest to the existence of Roman settlement – the legionaries' colony called **Mariana**. An Early Christian basilica and a 4th-century baptistry used to stand here before they were destroyed by the Lombards. After that the Mariana was threatened in turn by the Vandals, the Moors and by malaria – and it was finally abandoned in the 9th century.

Back again now to the N193, which continues on in the direction of Bonifacio and now becomes the N198. The second road to the right after the bridge over the Golo leads up to **Vescovato** in the Casinca. Just minutes away from the main coast road on the D6, this place is another world entirely. In a small square surrounded by plane trees, four ugly gargoyles spew out mountain water into a cast-iron fountain. Houses tower above, and here and there the odd trace of coloured plaster stands as a reminder of the time when this place took over the role of bishopric after Mariana had been abandoned, a secure refuge high above the perpetually-threatened plain.

After Venzolasca, turn right on the D6 towards **Loreto-di-Casinca**. This village, with its prominent campanile, seems close enough to touch, but keeps disappearing behind bends in the road. Soon Venzolasca lies far below, like a toy village, with the Lagoon of Biguglia spread out behind it. The predominantly old population of Loreto goes about its business: in the narrow road leading up to the *campanile*, doors stand wide open – little grocery shops that don't need name-boards because everyone knows everyone else.

Turn right along the D237 through the tiny villages of **Silvareccio** and **Piano** and towards the **Col Saint-Antoine**. You will notice that some of the slopes have chestnut trees on them. Formerly, chestnuts were used by the islanders to feed their animals, they were exchanged for oil and wine, they were *glacé* as *marrons de Nice*, and they were ground to make flour, or baked. Up on the pass (688m/ 2,250ft) behind the ivy and cypress trees on the right, stands the tower of the ruined monastery of **Saint-Antoine**. It was within these walls in 1755 – so a plaque next to the portal informs us – that Pasquale Paoli was appointed chief of the Corsican nation by a *consulta* shortly after his return from exile. Before you get to the fork in the pass, turn sharp left and carry on along the D515 to – according to the map – **Giocatojo**, which however now announces itself proudly as Ghjucatoghju. It lies on the edge of the **Parc Régional Naturel**, which was extended in 1992. The

Fountain in Loreto-di-Casinca

Village balcony

village is on a narrow ridge, with its church at the top. The road drops down through shady sections of forest alternating with sun-scorched clearings to reach the church square of **A Porta**. The clumsy restoration of the free-standing *campanile* next to the baroque church incurred the wrath of many a Corsican. But you can stop here for lunch, at the unpretentious restaurant **Elisabeth** (tel: 95392200) on the left of the iron fountain, which has a terrace jutting out over the valley below.

Hoar-frost, sometimes as late as Easter, and chestnut leaves and moss in autumn can make the roads around here slippery and treacherous. So even if you've calmly taken your time while sampling Corsican dishes in Elisabeth or in Piedicroce (**Le Refuge**), don't suddenly feel you need to hurry. Just before you reach Piedicroce on D71 you can see the tiny village of **Campana**, with its chapel above the road. The large painting behind the altar, an **Adoration of the Shepherds**, is a masterpiece of the Seville school and probably by Francisco Zurbarán (1598–1664). Ask for the key at the *mairie* opposite. Shortly after this on the left you can see the fenced-in ruins of the **Couvent d'Orezza**, a symbol of Corsican rejection of Genoese rule. It was here in 1731 that the islanders asked themselves whether a rebellion was in keeping with Christian teachings. Ten years later, in the same place, part of Paoli's constitution was passed. During the last battles on the island in 1944 the building, reduced to the role of an ammunition depot, was shot to pieces.

Man and herd

Down in the valley lies **Orezza**, once a spa resort with its own spring, now revived as a production centre of bubbly mineral water. At the entrance to the village of **Carcheto**, brown-coloured 'Parc Régional Naturel' signs point the way down to a waterfall and to the Church of **Santa Mar-**

garita. It's worth asking for the key here, too. The 15 naive pictures of the Stations of the Cross in the nave were painted by an unknown Castagniccia artist, who used foresters as models.

Continuing along the D71, you'll reach the highest point of this round trip at the **Col d'Arcarotta** (819m/2,700ft). Several villages can be seen far below on both sides; in the summertime the local craftsmen and smallholders hold a Sunday market up here. Over to the right, the huge **Punta di Caldane** (1,724m/5,650ft) blocks the way to the **Bozio** (*see Itinerary 6*). From this point it's downhill through the numerous hamlets of Felce. Further towards the sea, the landscape gets increasingly bare and desolate. Chiatra can be seen silhouetted against the reservoir at **Alesani**; its water is used to irrigate crops on the island's eastern plain.

The road now splits up again, with the left fork going off towards **Cervione**. This town, briefly the residence of King Theodore, has a depressing feel to it: even the finest of its buildings are falling to pieces, although the cathedral of Bishop Alexander, formerly known to the Corsicans as *Lisandru*, has been well restored. Just past it on the left the **Museu Etnugraficu** (open daily except Sundays and public holidays, 10am–noon and 2.30–6pm) will give you a good general impression of the history of the Castagniccia.

Where geraniums flourish

Another short detour before the coast leads along a narrow, seldom-used road that has been blasted out of the rock, in the direction of **San Nicolao**. From the stopping-places along here there are some excellent views to be had of the vineyards and citrus plantations on the flood-plain below. You pass a waterfall between two tunnels, and then the road winds its way on down to **Moriani Plage**. The sea is straight ahead, and you're on the 100-km (60-mile) long beach that stretches from Bastia to Solenzara. On the right-hand side of the passageway leading to the promenade, on the wall of an old fisherman's hut, you'll see a plaque: Ghjacinto Paoli sailed into exile in Italy from here, and in 1755 his son Pasquale came ashore to save the nation.

Bastia is an hour's drive northwards along the coast road.

Mountains & Villages

5. Corte and the Niolo

Through the Scala di Santa Regina and into the Niolo. A tour of the island's finest forests at the foot of Monte Cinto (2,710m/8,891ft). Then an afternoon stroll through the old part of Corte to the Citadel. See map on page 35.

Corte, the Corsicans' secret capital, is the perfect base for excursions into superb mountain scenery. But rather than staying in the town itself, I would suggest you try the **Hotel Colonna** at the entrance to the **Restonica Valley**, or there is a good bed-and-breakfast place right next to the mountain torrent a few hundred yards further on.

I would tend to leave the tour of the town itself till the afternoon, when the traffic has died down. After breakfast, drive through Corte and, after the bridge over the River Orta, take the D18 that branches off sharp left in a northerly direction. After around 20 minutes you'll find yourself at **Pont de Castirla**. If you want to eat here on your way back later on today it's best to reserve a table now in the restaurant on the right called **Chez Jacqueline**.

The ravine known as the **Scala di Santa Regina** begins on the other side of the Golo bridge, on the left. It is rough, full of bends, and at its upper end it used to be almost impos-

t hangs in the Scala de Santa Regina

sible to get through, making the Niolo valley basin virtually inaccessible until this road was completed in 1989. The ravine's name means 'staircase of the holy queen' and comes from the mule-path which used to wind its way over this massive threshold of reddish, almost bare granite in 17 huge bends. The river Golo descends 550m (1,800ft) between one end of the ravine and the other.

Then the valley suddenly broadens out, and you'll see the reservoir at the foot of the highest mountain on the island, **Monte Cinto** (2,710m/8,900ft). To the right, above Calacuccia, several villages are clustered across its southern slope, including the remote **Calasima** (1,095m/3,600ft), Corsica's highest village, above which the amazingly steep and jagged **Paglia Orba** (2,525m/8,300ft), known as 'Corsica's Matterhorn', dominates the view.

Even a valley basin as remote as this one was populated as long ago as the Stone Age. Beyond Calacuccia, between the L'Acqua Viva hotel-cum-filling station and the Le Corsica restaurant, you can see a weird-looking **dolmen** over to the left on a meadowy rise, and in the next village, **Albertacce**, there's a museum documenting all the finds in the region. The road now leads up towards the watershed to the southwest, passing through some of the finest forests on the island. The Laricio pine trees here are 40m (130ft) or more in height. Some of the really huge ones are as much as 600 years old, and they can measure up to 2m (6½ft) at the base. Their high tops create a lot of mysterious shade – probably the reason why the forest was named **Valdo Niello**, or 'Black Forest'.

The highest section of road on the island is the **Col de Vergio** (1,477m/4,850ft), marked by an enormous and very modern statue of Christ; the view from up here extends back across the Calacuccia Reservoir. On the other side of the pass the road then descends in a series of steep curves to Porto, on the west coast (*see Itinerary 12*).

On the way back, those feeling energetic might like to follow a 'Parc Naturel' sign that points the way down a side-road. It takes two hours from here to hike your way up to the beautifully-situated **Lac de Nino** (1,762m/5,780ft), the lake at the source of the Tavignano. Otherwise, at the end of the forest, just after the bridge over the river Golo, a road on the right leads off to **Casamaccioli**. This sleepy little village really

The defiant General Gaffori, Corte

Wild horses above Casamaccioli

wakes up on 8 September each year when the **A Santa di Niolo** is celebrated – the village's Festival of the Virgin. A procession follows a statue of Virgin and Child that is supposed to have been rescued from a monastery destroyed by the Turks in 1450. The monks, it is said, decided to let the statue choose its new sanctuary itself, and loaded it on to the back of a mule. Although the mule was not from the Niolo, he apparently trotted straight to Casamaccioli and stopped exactly where the church is today.

On the southern side of the lake, past the dam, your journey takes you back through the Scala di Santa Regina again. You can stop for lunch either at Chez Jacqueline or just before it at one of the two *auberges* inside the ravine itself. Remember, though, that you'll only make it back here by midday if you set off early enough and avoid the attractions of a walk in the forest along the way.

There is free parking in **Corte** past the Cours Paoli on the left, between the signposted turn-offs to the hospital and to Ajaccio. At the end of the Cours, you can see the large bronze statue of the famous freedom-fighter **Paoli** – paid for by 'grateful Corsica' in 1864. Behind it a steep flight of wide, flat steps covered with Tavignano gravel leads up to another statue: that of **General Gaffori**, standing with his back to his house. Its facade still bears traces of the famous siege by the Genoese.

A relief on the plinth of the statue relates the story of his courageous wife, Faustina. In 1746, her husband's men stormed the

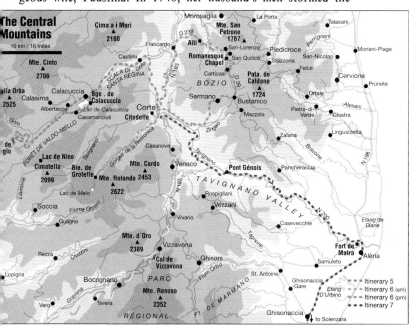

Citadel containing the Genoese who had managed to kidnap General Gaffori's young son. As they held him up to view on the battlements in order to obtain free passage, Faustina encouraged her compatriots to shoot all the same – the little boy remained unharmed. Four years later, the Genoese took advantage of Gaffori's absence to storm his home. The Corsican soldiers defending it were on the point of surrendering to the Genoese when Faustina, clutching a blunderbuss, walked over to some barrels of gunpowder and pointed it at them, saying she'd blow up the house with everyone in it rather than surrender. She thus gained valuable time before reinforcements arrived.

Gaffori's outstretched arm points off to the left in the direction of the artisans' quarter and the **Belvedere**, a small platform with a view down to the city and up to the Citadel. To reach the main gate of the latter, climb up some more steps on the right-hand side of the Place Gaffori. Here, you'll pass by the birthplace of Napoleon's brother Joseph, who later became king of Spain and Naples, and also the **Palais National** (Palazzu Naziunale), seat of the government of Corsica from 1755 to 1769. The long, crumbling Citadel is undergoing a new lease of life: there is an **information office** just past the main gate; opposite, the Parc Naturel provides details of its hiking routes *(service randonnées)*; art exhibitions are held here; and the Citadel also contains various institutes forming part of the University of Corsica, situated just below the town. Though founded in 1765 by Paoli, the university was only reopened in 1982.

At the northern end of the square in front of the Citadel, steps lead down to the **Fontaine des Quatre Canons** and then on to the Cours Paoli. **La Bohème** brasserie, situated between the two routes up to the Citadel, offers a menu catering for all tastes – including a delicious and very good-value *Menu Corse*.

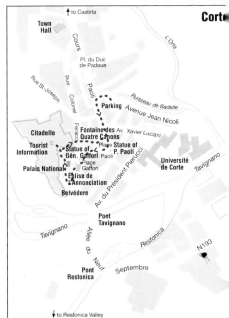

6. Two Mountain Worlds

By car through the Gorges de la Restonica and a morning hike up to the Melo mountain lake (1,711m/5,600ft). Then, a round trip through the villages of the Bozio, on the other side of the Castagniccia. See map on page 35.

Follow the signs to the **Gorges de la Restonica** along the D623 from Corte. The road starts off nice and smooth, but soon becomes bumpy and narrow, and a series of hairpins takes you ever higher above the mountain river, across stone bridges devoid of any kind of parapet. In some places there's hardly room for two cars to pass. There are plans to close this road to private cars altogether, and just use minibuses.

The Gorges de la Restonica

In contrast to the almost completely bare Scala di Santa Regina, this ravine has chestnut trees and Laricio pine dotted across its ochre-coloured rocky walls. About two-thirds of the way along, the road switches over to the right bank, and soon the trees are far behind you. The car park at the **Bergeries de Grottelle** (1,375m/ 4,500ft), a group of shepherds' huts, is another 45 minutes' drive away.

The journey continues on foot. Sturdy footwear and an anorak, even in summer, are essential. The hiking trail is marked by orange and yellow signs at first, and after half an hour's walk the two colours split up. **Yellow** leads off to the right with the warning *accès difficile* – a demanding route, in other words, with several steep sections. The **orange** paint-marks lead off to the left, to an *accès facile*, which takes you round in a big circle through alder groves as far as the **Lac de Melo** (1,711m/5,600ft), one of the seven mountain lakes surrounding **Monte Rotondo** (2,622m/8,600ft), which you can see towering off to the left. In summer, the meadows here are full of flowers. The hike to the lake and back takes between two and three hours, and back at the car park the shepherds will sell you cold drinks and enormous sandwiches containing smoked meat or goat's cheese. The **Relais du Lac**, along the road on the other side of the bridge, also serves delicious trout straight from the mountain stream.

The lunch break will give you ample time to relax before you make an afternoon visit to the area northeast of Corte known as the **Bozio** (U Boziu). This is the back door, as it were, of the Castagniccia (*see Itinerary 4*), and is hardly ever visited by tourists. From Corte, take the N193 in the direction of Bastia. In **Francardo**, the D239 to **Aiti** branches off to the right at a chapel just past the Rex Bar; a less narrow and more comfortable alternative here would be to travel 4km (2 miles) or so further on, and when you're almost at the end of a straight stretch of road, to take the D39 over a bridge across the river Golo. The drive up to Aiti, though, with its seemingly endless hairpin bends, has a treat in store: opposite the tiny village, on the other side of the valley, you will gain a superb view of **Mt San Petrone** (1,767m/5,800ft) and of the rough mountain ridge in front of the Castagniccia.

You now descend steeply. On the other side of the bridge across the Casaluna, turn sharp right onto the D39, in the direction of Cambia and Carticasi. Beyond San Lorenzo, between Corsoli and Cambia, a signpost points the way to **San Quilico**, with its Romanesque chapel containing 16th-century frescoes. The road comes to an end in this tiny hamlet, where you'll see a wooden arrow pointing straight down, bearing the inscription *L'intérieur ne se visite pas*. Nevertheless, the short descent is worth it just for a chance to see the wall paintings here. The little chapel's front and side entrances have symbolic figures carved into the stone that are reminiscent of similar ones at San Michele near Murato and the Trinità near Aregno (*see Itinerary 13*). Eve can be seen taking the apple of temptation from the serpent's mouth, and there is also a figure wearing a belt – St Michael, perhaps – clutching a dragon-like serpent with his left hand and drawing a short sword with his right. The odd thing about this remote little building is that it wasn't constructed until 1576; the purely Pisan architectural style seems to have lasted far longer in this very remote area.

The church in Sermano

Beyond the pass above **Bustanico**, the Bozio suddenly opens up to the south, soaking up the warmth of the sun even in the cooler months of the year. The view now stretches far across the Tavignano basin to the **Monte d'Oro** and **Monte Rotondo** near the Lac de Melo. The uprising against the Genoese broke out in Bustanico in 1729, when a tax-collector deprived an old man of his very last penny, and finally ended four whole decades later when the island was subjugated by the French. Bustanico's parish church, just below the main road through the village, contains a very impressive 18th-century crucifix, carved by an unknown local artist. The next village you come to, **Sermano**, has, along with the village of Rusio, kept up the ancient tradition of the *paghjella* in its religious festivals (see *Calendar of Events*). Thanks to these two villages, this polyphonic form of singing has been given a new lease of life. As you descend towards the Tavignano in the late afternoon, you can see **Castellare-di-Mercurio**, on its narrow outcrop, silhouetted against the mountain scenery. Back down in the valley once more, turn right. Corte is just 6km (4 miles) away.

7. Corte to Bonifacio

From Corte, through the Tavignano Valley, to the ancient ruins of Aléria. Along the east coast to the primeval fortress of Arraggio (Arraghju) near Porto-Vecchio, and then past some fine beaches to Bonifacio. See maps on pages 35 and 45.

This route has several longish stretches, but also fewer stops. It takes you from the northern to the southern half of the island. In Corte, follow the white arrow to **Aléria** before you reach the railway station, and after the roundabout go under a bridge and join the N200 which follows the Tavignano down towards the east coast. After a quarter of an hour, the road swings across a Genoese-built bridge to the north bank of the river. The bridge is very solidly-built: its three stone arches have not only withstood the mountain torrents for centuries, but have also survived the strains of motor traffic. On the other side is the equally solidly-built **Chapel of Saint-Jean-Baptiste**, dating from the 10th century. It was used as a refuge by shepherds for generations, and contains several ornamental inscriptions.

The foothills of the Castagniccia now force the Tavignano, and

The Genoese bridge

with it the road as well, down into a winding ravine, and then the valley opens up to reveal the coast. In **Cateraggio** turn right on to the N198, and from the bridge over the Tavignanu, the little village of Aléria can already be seen on the higher bank opposite. Towering above it is the **Fort de Matra**, which today houses the **Musée Jérôme Carcopino**, containing all the archaeological finds from the excavations on the flood-plain. There are relics here dating from the Stone, Bronze and Ice Ages, and also some fine Greek vases that were found in the necropolis at the foot of the plateau, showing Bacchic and erotic scenes. The Carthaginians left some blown glass behind, the Etruscans left several drinking-horns shaped like dogs' and mules' heads, and the Roman exhibits are mostly practical: coins, oil-lamps and amphorae. The remains of the **Roman city of Aléria**, which in its heyday had a population of 20,000, are situated on a plateau to the southwest of the village.

Near the mouth of the Tavignano river, the **Etang de Diane** forms a natural harbour, which the Romans used as their naval base. From here, grain, olive-oil, honey, wine, cork-bark, fish and mussels from the lagoon were shipped off to Rome, just one day away by boat. Oysters were also transported, salted, in amphorae. Today, sea bass *(loup)* and kingfish are also bred here as well as in the **Etang d'Urbino**, somewhat further to the south. On both lagoons you can have your food fished out for you on the spot, at restaurants situated directly at the water's edge.

After your delicious seafood meal, it takes another half-hour to get to **Solenzara** (Sulinzara). If you feel the urge to get back into the mountains at this point, you can take an 80-km (50-mile) trip up to the **Col de Bavella** (1,218m/3,990ft) with its crenellated ridges, reminiscent of the Dolomites. You'll be getting almost a finer view of it though – from a bit further away and from its other side – if you follow *Itinerary 9*.

The excavations at Aléria

The afternoon today can thus be spent in a more relaxing and equally interesting manner down near the coast.

Around 20km (12 miles) beyond Solenzara, the D559, closely followed by the D759, branches off in the direction of **Arraghju**. Brown 'Parc Naturel' signs lead you to a house with a car park on its left, and a sign to **Castellu** on its right. Walk across the courtyard, then cross some stepping-stones over a stream, and after a very steep 20-minute climb you'll finally reach your destination: a round fortress made of reddish stone, situated imposingly on a small rise. It is one of the largest and most intact Torréen fortresses, whose structure even contains a basin for collecting rainwater, built into the rock. The view from here extends from the **Golfe de la Pinarellu** as far as the **Golfe de Porto-Vecchio**.

Take a break

As you enter **Porto-Vecchio** (Porti-Vecchju), follow the signs to the harbour *(Port)* at the roundabout just outside the town. If the traffic doesn't look too bad you could also risk driving directly to the centre, and through the **Porte Genoise**. There are parking spaces at the Hôtel de Ville or further down on either side of the main exit to Bastia. The **Place de L'Eglise**, surrounded by cafés, is very charming, and from the Porte Genoise there is a view of the salt production area on the other side of the harbour. Otherwise the town isn't all that attractive, and doesn't have any memorable sights.

Shortly after the exit in the direction of Bonifacio a sign on the left points the way towards **Palombaggia**. Its beaches, framed by red cliffs and broad, shady pine-trees, lie at the end of a small side-road opposite the **Iles Cerbicale**. Out of season, this place is a dream. However, the collection of villas, bungalow villages and apartments on the slopes gives you a good idea of the sheer crush it can become at some times of the year.

Bonifacio, the destination for today, is just half an hour away, along the *route nationale*. When you arrive, you'll notice that down by the quay there is one-way traffic – in the opposite direction. Park on the left or the right before you reach the harbour, therefore, or drive up a steep hill, then down a bit, then up again through a short tunnel to the upper part of the town, where there are more parking spaces. There are three new hotels now in the Old Town, equipped with every modern convenience: **Le Genovese** up on the corner of the inlet, the three-star **Le Roy d'Aragon** down at the quayside and between them, halfway up the upper part of the town, **Le Royal**. The latter is very good value.

The South

8. Bonifacio

Through the narrow streets of the Citadel, and up to the former batteries high above the ocean. Then a journey by boat along the steep coastline, either to the grottoes or to the Lavezzi Islands.

There's something very un-Corsican about **Bonifacio** (Bonifaziu). Built as a bastion against Moorish raids, it seems almost African. It could be the white limestone cliffs that make the light here so much more intense.

The upper part of the town naturally has no need of a defensive wall on its seaward side: at the end of the broad Montée Rastello, with its flat steps, next to the **Oratoire Saint-Roch**, stepping up to the parapet is quite a shock. Sixty metres (200ft) below, the sea crashes onto the rocks; up on your right the Old Town sticks out over the abyss like a seagull's nest. And far off, on the other side of the **Straits of Bonifacio**, the bluish, hazy coastline of Sardinia can be seen shimmering in the distance.

The fortifications begin above Saint-Roch, at the **Belvedere de la Manichella**. The Montée Saint-Roch, gaining height all the time, leads to it through a drawbridge which provided the only means of access until well into the 19th century. On the harbour side

Bonifacio is perched on the cliffs

One way of getting around

the wall of the Citadel drops away unbelievably steeply; it used to enclose the upper town as far as the round tower high above the sea called the **Torrione**. The inhabitants here were always well-equipped to withstand sieges – the one by the King of Aragon in 1420 lasted five months.

On the **Place d'Armes**, you can see round lids that used to cover large grain silos hewn out of the limestone below, and at the Torreone, the **Bartolomeo Well** extended more than 70m (230ft) down to a spring below sea-level. Legend has it that the stone staircase leading down to the sea from up here, with its 187 steps, was carved out of the rock by soldiers from Aragon in just one night.

The 14th-century Church of **Sainte-Marie-Majeure** has a highly ornamental tower and also a loggia – a roofed courtyard with an arcade – where the city elders used to hold their meetings. Inside the church, a 3rd-century Roman sarcophagus made of marble once served as a font, and the tabernacle (1465) is also a rare treat.

If you now continue on towards the tip of the peninsula on which the Citadel is situated you'll pass the rather theatrical **Foreign Legion Monument**, which once used to stand in the North African town of Saida. The Legion itself occupied the western side of the rock until 1983, and left it completely desolate. The only troops here now are a detachment of army rangers. The round towers, recently restored, were once windmills; casemates and cannon emplacements were combined closely with the Genoese bastions. They now form part of an interesting route to stroll along, providing views down to the harbour entrance, and the **La Madonetta lighthouse** in front of it. Next to the Montlaur barracks, **Saint-Dominique** can be seen with its octagonal tower and battlements. It is the only Gothic church on the island, and very severe in style. Several *chasses* – processional figures carried about during Easter Week, some of them incredibly heavy – are kept here.

Down on the **Quai Comparetti**, fishing-boats and yachts lie anchored directly in front of a row of restaurants and cafés, with

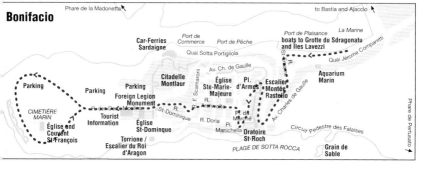

menus and snacks to suit every size of wallet. An **aquarium** – its contents supplied by the local fishermen – gives a glimpse of the marine life along this stretch of the coast. People even dive for coral here – it grows at depths of 60m (200ft) or more – and a craft enterprise at the bottom of the Montée Rastello uses it to make beautiful jewellery.

One adventurous thing to do here is to take a boat trip out of the harbour, past the town, up to the enormous 'Grain of Sand' rock and into the blue depths of the **Grotte du Sdragonatu**. The journey takes just over an hour. Give yourself a bit longer, though, if you want to visit the **Iles Lavezzi**, a paradise of an archipelago composed of windswept and water-eroded rocks out in the Straits. If the weather gets stormy this series of flattish cliffs can be absolute hell. The frigate **La Sémillante** was wrecked here during a fog in 1855 on its way to the Crimea. All 750 people on board perished. The victims who were washed ashore lie buried in three of the island's graveyards.

9. Stones that Speak

A journey west from Bonifacio past some natural rock formations, then back inland to Sartène and to the primeval fortresses at Cucuruzzu and Capula. An afternoon side-trip to the megalithic site of Filitosa.

Just to the north of Bonifacio, the N196 branches off to the left towards Sartène and Ajaccio. Very soon, over on the right you can

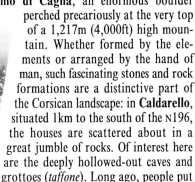

see the **Uomo di Cagna**, an enormous boulder perched precariously at the very top of a 1,217m (4,000ft) high mountain. Whether formed by the elements or arranged by the hand of man, such fascinating stones and rock formations are a distinctive part of the Corsican landscape: in **Caldarello**, situated 1km to the south of the N196, the houses are scattered about in a great jumble of rocks. Of interest here are the deeply hollowed-out caves and grottoes (*taffone*). Long ago, people put

The lion of Roccapina

windows and doors into the openings, and they were inhabited until as recently as the 17th century. Today they are used as stables and store-rooms.

A short while later, at the top of a small pass, your gaze will be drawn to a weird rock formation straight ahead – the **Lion of Roccapina**. The beast seems to be enjoying a comfortable siesta on a rocky outcrop above the sea; a few kilometres further on, at the **Auberge Coralli**, a narrow track leads up to this odd formation. The 'lion' lies above a very beautiful, protected beach. From here you can

Sartène

clearly see that its 'mane' is artificial, and is actually made up of the crumbling ruins of what once used to be a coastal fortress.

Another place that seems to be part of the rock it stands on is **Sartène** (Sartè), or at least its old town. This 'most Corsican of Corsican towns', as Prosper Mérimée, author of *Carmen* and *Colomba*, described it in 1839, has been spoiled somewhat by all the contemporary architecture now surrounding its medieval core.

The best way to park is to drive down and then turn sharp left beneath the town wall. Walk past the **Echauguette**, a small 12th-century projecting bastion, then past the post office and after a brief ascent you'll soon find yourself in the town's shady central square, the **Place Porta.** Through a gate beneath the *mairie* (formerly the Genoese governor's palace), a few more steps will transport you into the medieval atmosphere of the **Manighedda Quarter.** The passages, alleyways and stone staircases here are almost entirely devoid of light, and run between houses built of rough slabs of masonry, some of them eight storeys high.

This dimly-lit *milieu* was the breeding-ground for the *Vendetta*. Drawn into the feuds between the all-powerful landowners, different quarters of the town would do battle with each other at the slightest provocation. It was only in 1834 that a contract signed in the Church of **Santa-Maria** put an end to the fighting. This gruesome past also goes a long way towards explaining the rite of the **Cate-**

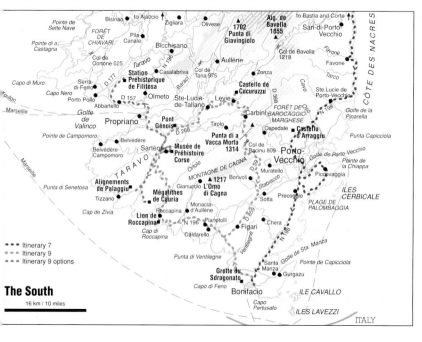

● ● ● Itinerary 7
● ● ● Itinerary 9
● ● ● Itinerary 9 options

The South

16 km / 10 miles

One of life's pleasures – good conversation

nacciu – the name given to an anonymous penitent wearing a red cowl with slits for the eyes, with a 14-kg (31lb) chain attached to his ankle, who on Good Friday shoulders a massive cross weighing 31kg (68lb) and carries it through the town barefoot (*see Calendar of Events*).

Off to the right above the Place Porta, the town's former prison houses the **Musée de Préhistoire Corse** (open daily except weekends 10am–noon and 2–4pm). A visit here will stand you in good stead for the afternoon.

At this point you can fortify yourself with a snack in one of the *brasseries* on the Place Porta or a proper lunch at the **Auberge Santa Barbara** below the city, in the direction of Propriano. However, if you want to experience the highlight of this afternoon's trip – the Stone Age fortress at Cucuruzzu – in all its glory without anyone else around, it's best to have a picnic handy and to use this quiet time for travelling. Follow the road downhill out of Sartène in the direction of **Propriano** (Pruprià), turn off right after 6km (4 miles) along the D268. After about 3km (2 miles) you can stop briefly on the right at a lay-by to admire the elegance of the Genoese bridge known as the **Spin'a Cavallu** (horse's back) over the Rizzanese. About half an hour later you'll reach **Ste Lucie-de-Tallano**, and it's worth stopping briefly here, too, in the square with its war memorial, because the plinth of the statue is made of a stone that is very rare indeed. It is a type of diorite that can only be found in one private quarry on Corsica, and also in Finland: *diorit orbiculaire*.

Continue on now in the direction of Levie until you see a sign just after the Cumuna di Mela on the left, pointing the way towards the **Sites Archéologiques de Levie** at **Cucuruzzu** and **Capula**. After about 10 minutes the road ends up at a car park. A small stone information booth points the way to the most fascinating primeval fortresses on the island, alongside Arraghju (*see Itinerary 7*). Cucuruzzu is a 15 minutes' walk, Capula is 20 minutes more from there and it takes 15 minutes more to get back to your starting point. The path passes through bizarre rock formations and giant, moss-covered trees, the whole place like an enchanted forest.

Cucuruzzu was built around 1500BC, during the Bronze Age, on a natural rock formation. There are 'Parc Naturel' signs explaining how the place was constructed. From the walls the view across to the **Aiguilles de Bavella** (1,596m/5,200ft) is superb. The site was finally abandoned in the 3rd century BC, but the Bronze Age fortress at Capula was extended several times and was used as a refuge by the island's *Seigneurs* as late as the 13th century – which is why it looks so much more 'modern'. Details of the sites are clearly documented at the **Musée Archéologique** in Levie (open daily except Sunday, 10am–noon and 3–7pm as well as 2–6pm in winter). The oldest lady in Corsica can be seen lying here too, in a coffin: the skeleton of the 'Lady of Bonifacio', who died 8,500 years ago at the age of 35, probably from rheumatism. A 15th-century ivory crucifix of the Donatello school can also be seen in the *mairie* during weekday office hours; telephone first to announce your visit (tel: 9957 84015).

An enchanted landscape

You can now take the D59 to **Carbini** with its free-standing *campanile*, visible for miles around. Built in the late 11th century, it is probably the oldest bell-tower on the island. The Church of **San Giovanni** next to it is also Pisan. A rebellion began here in the 14th century: the sect of the Giovannali, who threatened the order of the church and the *seigneurs* by demanding equality, were eventually accused of debauchery and put to death by papal soldiers inside the church. From Carbini you can then take the D59/859 past Sotta and via Figari, before rejoining the N196 to Bonifacio.

An alternative for the afternoon, particularly if you're heading up to Ajaccio, is to visit the megalithic site of **Filitosa**, home to the island's most impressive collection of statue-menhirs. From Sartène continue along the N196, drive around the outside of **Propriano** and about 5km (3 miles) further on, where the N196 goes round a large hairpin, turn down to the left on to the D157 and travel along the coast in the direction of Porto Pollo. You'll already notice the signs to Filitosa, which is situated on a slope above the broad valley of the Taravu. You need to buy a ticket at the restaurant by the entrance: the site is actually on private property (open daily 8am–8pm, or until dusk).

The original inhabitants of the island, the Corsi, sculpted the statues; some in their own image and some in the image of the ultimately victorious Torréen invaders. Only a few steps into the site, you're confronted by a grim-looking menhir-guard, armed with dagger and sword: this is the Torréen menhir known as **Filitosa** v. The menhir heads you come across next, **Filitosa** vi to xi and xii, lined up in a row by the excavation teams on the round wall of the central monument, actually look the most peace-loving of the lot, and only a few fragments betray the odd breast-plate or weapon. These were probably ritual steles created by the Corsi before the arrival of the Torréens. The invaders smashed them and used the fragments to help build their *torre*. The tower-like West Monument, high above the valley, was also used by the Corsi. Down below, further menhirs were also placed to form a partial circle: **Filitosa** i to iv and also **Tappa** i. Seen from above they appear very lifelike indeed, and as you walk down to them they reveal features very different from those of their 'colleagues' above. **Filitosa** i wears a sword in his belt, **Filitosa** iii and iv each have a dagger, number ii has very clearly sculpted shoulder-blades, and **Tappa** i, although shaped like a person, could also be construed as a phallic symbol.

There are more sculptures in the small museum just before the exit: **Scalsa Murta** (circa 1400bc) was found in very good condition; with its helmet and its muscular chest, it can be seen standing alongside **Filitosa** xii and **Tappa** ii. The depressions in the helmets were probably there to accommodate cattle-horns.

Other statue-menhirs in the south of the island can be seen at the Alignements de Palaggiu and the Mégalithes de Cauria, both to the south of Sartène. They, too, represent the victors and the vanquished. It wasn't only the Torréens who smashed the likenesses of themselves and their victims; the Christians, too, used the statues as construction material to help build their churches, having duly exorcised them first (*see Itinerary 11*).

If you have visited the site at Filitosa, I suggest you round off the day with a swim at **Abartello**, directly opposite Propriano.

Among the menhirs of Filitosa

The West Coast

10. Ajaccio

From the morning market to Napoleon's birthplace and his various statues. Visits to the Chapelle Impériale and the Musée Fesch. Sunset from the Iles Sanguinaires.

In Bastia they work, in Ajaccio they take it easy. This part-derogatory, part-envious saying is actually truer the other way round. In **Ajaccio** (Aiacciu) the regional parliament looks after politics and concentrates on lobbying the central government in Paris, which can make life rather hectic at times. But above all else, Ajaccio is imbued with the aura of the island's greatest son, **Napoleon**. It's less of an aura these days, actually – more like an enormous neon sign, and there's no getting away from the posthumous fame of the dubious Bonaparte clan. It's not only the statues and

Napoleon with his brothers on the Place Diamant

the historic sites, either: apart from all the souvenir kitsch, a cinema has been named after him and he has even been used to help market light-bulbs, which can be seen dangling above the streets like Christmas decorations throughout the entire year.

The first thing you need to do in this rather chaotic town is to find some relatively peaceful accommodation (*see Practical Information*). If you're just passing through, parking is available beneath the **Place Diamant** (its real name is actually Place de Gaulle), and at the harbour ferry in front of the market in the **Square César Campinchi**. From here you can reach all the town's sights on foot.

The **morning market** here is more colourful and luxurious than its equivalent in Bastia. In the adjoining building complex, facing the sea, is the **fish hall**; the other side of the same building faces the Place Foch and contains the Office de Tourisme, the Town Hall and, on the first floor, a **Musée Napoléonien**. Here you can see a marble statue of Jérôme Bonaparte, King of Westphalia, wearing a Roman toga, pointing the way towards the *Grand Salon* with its portraits and busts, Napoleon's birth certificate written in Genoese Italian (a photocopy), and his death mask cast in bronze. In the direction of the town centre, at the end of the Place Foch, beneath the plane trees and palms, you can see Napoleon himself as **Premier Consul** keeping an eye on the Four Lions Fountain. The small statue of the Virgin set into a façade across to the left, known as **A Madonnuccia,** is supposed to have protected the town from the plague in 1656; it certainly seems to have done more for Ajaccio than Napoleon ever did.

The Rue Bonaparte leads past this house on the corner and up towards the Citadel (closed to visitors), and in the third street to the right you'll find **Napoleon's birthplace,** the **Casa**. Back in 1769 the building was by no means as elegant as it is now. Laeticia, Napoleon's *Madame Mère* from Sartène, only managed to do it up with the help of compensation after it had been virtually demolished by the British and the Paolists. In the small garden opposite you can see the bust of the Roi de Rome when he was still a child, the son of the Emperor and Marie-Louise of Austria. He was meant to become Napoleon II, but achieved fame as the Duke of Reichstadt. The sedan chair in the *entrée* to the Casa is the one Laeticia is supposed to have been carried home in from church when she felt her first labour pains – the furniture inside the building is even less authentic and altogether rather gaudy.

Something far closer to the average Corsican's heart can be found if you go up the Rue Saint-Charles a short way and go left and then right, to reach the Cathedral of **Notre-Dame-de-la-Miséricorde**. Through the portal on the right, in a niche behind a small grating, you can see the font, and a red marble plaque on a pillar

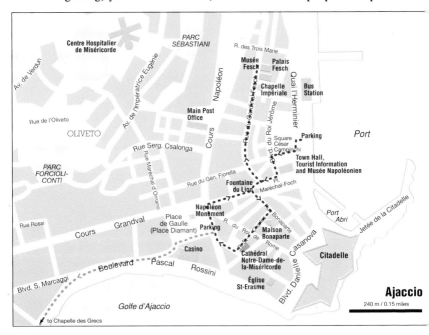

to the left attests to Napoleon's desire to be buried in his native city. However, when he died on St Helena in 1821 he no longer belonged to his island; he was far too famous by then, and was buried not in the imperial tomb at Ajaccio, but under the dome of Les Invalides in Paris.

You will see Napoleon again, up on horseback this time, wearing golden laurels, staring across the Place Diamant and surrounded by four regal personages on foot: his brothers Joseph, Lucien, Louis and Jérôme. And at the end of the long avenue leading away from the Four Lions Fountain, you can see him yet again in one of his typical poses, with the fingers of his left hand thrust inside his jacket. The ramp proudly displaying all the names of his military victories is used today as a slide by children from the nearby blocks of flats. The young Bonaparte is meant to have played in a grotto at the back on the left.

The **Chapelle Impériale** in the Rue Fesch contains the remains of his parents, a few family members and Cardinal Fesch, a stepbrother of Laeticia's, the art-loving archbishop of Lyons, who collected around 16,000 paintings, mostly by Italian masters. The chapel forms the south wing of the **Palais Fesch**, in whose courtyard a bronze statue shows the cardinal with his hand placed rather hypocritically on his heart. Although the ravages of time have left only about a thousand of his paintings in Ajaccio, these do make up what is considered to be the third most important collection of 14th–18th-century Italian works in the world, after those in the Uffizi in Florence and the Louvre in Paris. Among the works on display in the renovated building (opening hours vary, see *Museums* under *Practical Information*) are a triptych from the **Rimini school** and several paintings by Giotto, Botticelli, Bellini, Titian, Caravaggio and Veronese.

Napoleon's ramp

In the evening, why not do as Napoleon did while still a young man? He used to walk westwards as far as the **Chapelle des Grecs** along the Rue des Sanguinaires. Before or after enjoying an evening apéritif at one of the cafés on the seafront boulevard de Lantivy, depending on the time of year, you too can travel 12km (7½ miles) westwards to the **Pointe de la Parata** and watch the sun sink down behind the Iles Sanguinaires.

Beauty on the beach

11. Ajaccio to Porto

Busy and deserted beaches. The 'Greek' town of Cargèse. A 'work of the devil': the Calanche Rocks. The Gulf of Porto, now a national monument under UNESCO protection.

Follow the N194 northeastwards out of Ajaccio. The quickest route to the north of the island and Calvi would actually involve continuing along the main road via the central mountains, Corte and Ile Rousse – but that would mean missing out on the best and most spectacular part of the west coast, so I suggest you turn left at Mezzavia, after about 4km (2½ miles), following the sign which reads 'par la côte'.

Once you've crossed the threshold separating Ajaccio from its hinterland you can see the Bay of Lava down below on the left, after which you reach the top of the pass known as the **Bocca di San Bastiano** (411m/1,350ft). Beyond it you can see the Cinarca rising above the Golfe de Sagone. Like the Balagne (*see Itineraries 13 and 14*), the Cinarca, too, was once a very fertile landscape. Long after the arable land to the north *(Terra di u cummune)* had been partitioned equally and justly, the Cinarca was still under the yoke of the feudal *Seigneurs*. Its valleys facing the sea are now prospering economically, thanks to the tourist boom on the coast.

The first large bay you will reach, the **Golfe de la Liscia** between Ancone and Tiuccia, is packed with villas and holiday villages. This all suddenly changes the moment you round the Genoese tower at the Punta di Capigliolo. The long, gently-curving beach on either side of the **Liamone Estuary** is still wild and unspoilt. Its first half is almost completely bare, and beyond the river it is bordered by an area of bush. Just the place for a longish morn-

The coast road near Porto

ing swim, though when the wind gets the surf up the current here can get pretty dangerous. Nevertheless, Ajaccio's only about an hour behind you, and you can take your time. Sagone or Cargèse are good places for lunch, and neither is far away.

The left turn out of Sagone will take you along the beach and at the end of this short, straight section of road on the right, just after you cross the bridge over the Sagone river, you'll see a near-ruin standing about 90m (300ft) away. This used to be the 12th-century episcopal **Cathedral of Sant' Appiano**. Its foundations are far older: they date from the 4th century. Directly above the site, a menhir can be clearly seen, acting as a cornerstone.

Cargèse lies a 15-minute drive to the west, and is situated high above the sea. It was founded by around 600 Greeks from the Peloponnese town of Vitylo, on the run from Turkish occupation. They first settled a bit further up the slope in 1676 and named their community Paomia. Their successful attempts at agriculture combined with their loyalty to Genoa, however, soon incurred the envy and the wrath of the Corsicans. In 1732 they were driven from their homes by the people living in the mountains near Vico. After suffering two periods of exile in Ajaccio, they were finally allowed home again for good in 1793 during the French occupation of the island.

Today reminders of the area's Greek origins can be found in the surnames of the local population, many of which end in -*polis* or -*dacci* (from -*dakis*), and in the local white Greek Orthodox church. This stands opposite

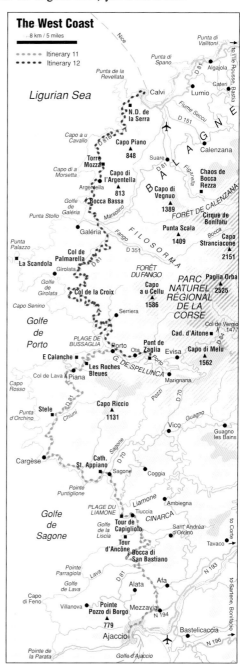

The West Coast

8 km / 5 miles

- - - - - Itinerary 11
■■■■■ Itinerary 12

a very Corsican-looking church, constructed by members of the local parish in 1870, which contains a whole wealth of icons, some of them from Mount Athos. Mass here is celebrated by the same priest, who wears different raiments depending on which church he happens to be in.

Halfway to **Piana**, on a bend in the road beyond a bridge, a stele can be seen commemorating the island's liberation at the end of 1942. Officers who had come ashore from the submarine *Casabianca* met leaders of the Corsican resistance movement for initial discussions, and distributed weapons.

The road now winds its way across countryside that is almost completely uninhabited, until you suddenly see the whole **Golfe de Porto** from the **Col de Lava** (498m/1,600ft) just before reaching Piana. This gulf, with its red porphyritic rocks, is now one of the world's national monuments under UNESCO protection. Its most spectacular section begins rather suddenly at a bridge over a mountain stream beyond Piana: **E Calanche**. For years, Corsican shepherds called it a 'work of the devil': a rough and bizarrely-shaped mass of rock, almost like flames stretching down into the sea, and throwing blue shadows at dusk, with contours reminiscent of mythical creatures and monsters. You can reach some of these rock formations, the 'Eagle' or the 'Tortoise' for instance – and they aren't scary at all during the day – by going up the path next to the bridge beyond the **Chalet des Roches Bleues**. Three-quarters of an hour later the path, quite steep at first, leads back to the main road. A bit further down, on a sharp curve, the hour-long alternative route heads off via the 'dog's head' *(tête de chien)* to a natural 'château' with a good view down to the village of Porto.

Porto is guarded by its square tower

In the old days **Porto** used to be nothing more than a tiny fishing harbour belonging to the mountain village of **Ota**, situated 4½km (2½ miles) inland. Porto was one of the first places on the island to be developed into a tourist centre. UNESCO protection arrived rather late, but has ensured that the local red stone is used for all new housing projects so a natural atmosphere is retained. Once you've chosen a hotel for the night from the huge selection available, there's still time to go for a swim on the pebble beach in front of the eucalyptus grove. The water here sometimes bubbles like champagne.

A brief walk in the Gorges de Spelunca. Then two mountain passes with superb views across the Golfe de Girolata, and finally a trip to a castle just outside Calvi, that was once owned by a member of the Bonaparte family. See map on page 53.

The Genoese bridge at Ota

The Porto River reaches the sea calmly, almost dreamily, at a beach below a recently restored Genoese tower, blown apart long ago. Just a few kilometres upriver, though, it consists of a whole series of torrents thundering down from the alpine watershed. The ones that have cut deepest into the rock here are the Tavulella and the Aitone, forming the **Gorges de Spelunca**. The old mule track to the mountain village of Evisa passes through these gorges, and going uphill the whole way would take at least three hours. However, a short walk in the lowest part of the gorge gives you a very good idea of what the island's former 'road system' used to be like.

First of all, drive to **Ota**. There are legends galore about the Sphinx-shaped rock high above the village: according to one of them, two hermits up there have been restraining the rock for centuries with the aid of hemp ropes. On the other side of the village the road descends to the entrance to the gorge, and just before it on the right you can see a well-preserved Genoese bridge spanning the Porto river. The footpath into the gorge – part of the **Tra mare e monti** hiking trail – begins on the right at the new double road bridge, and leads you alongside the mountain stream for three-quarters of an hour until it reaches a second Genoese hump-backed bridge, the **Pont de Zaglia**, where the Tavulella and the Aitone join forces. This is where you turn back.

Lunch or a picnic can be combined with a swim on the pebble beach at **Bussaglia**; roughly 5km (3 miles) to the north of Porto, a short side-road off the D81 will take you down there. After this you come to the section of road with more curves than anywhere else on this coastal route. Stop briefly at the **Col de la Croix**, 272m (890ft) above the Golfe de Girolata. The fort and several houses belonging to the

Snack on the Col de la Croix

village of **Girolata** can be seen from here. The village itself can only be reached either by a very bothersome mule track, or by boat from Porto or Calvi.

In order to reach the **Col de Palmarella** on the opposite side – 4½km (2½ miles) as the crow flies – the road has to zig-zag its way 11½km (over 7 miles) along the slopes. The other pass is higher up (406m/1,300ft), and the view across the bay, framed by mountains, is unforgettable.

The road winds its way down quickly, around innumerable bends and through a lot of *macchia*, to reach the **Fango** valley. The river-bed here is usually dry. It's only the valley's unusual width and the amount of scree on either side of it that betray the huge masses of water that crash through here on their way to the sea nearby whenever the snow thaws, or during heavy rainstorms. A stone bridge with five arches leads you to the other bank. Upriver, you can see the **Paglia Orba** (*see Itinerary 5*), which looks a lot more like the Matterhorn from here than it did from the Niolo side. If you turn right here and travel inland on the D81 you can gain half an hour on the way to Calvi. The left turn, though – the D81B – is much more beautiful. You pass two black beaches down below on the left; one opposite Galeria and the other at Argentella.

On a hill in front of the mountains, its windows empty and looking very solitary indeed, stands what is left of **Torre Mozza**. Not a watchtower, but instead the all-too-brief dream of a member of the Bonaparte family who was keen on the Romantic 'back-to-nature' movement. Politics also played a role. Prince Pierre Napoleon, a nephew of the Emperor (the son of his brother Lucien), moved out here at the age of 38 when his ambitions suffered a blow: his cousin Louis was named imperial heir. His only consolation was to return to the land of his forefathers, and he lived for several years in this wilderness, also known as the **Balagne Déserte**, eight hours' ride from Calvi, until he and his mistress Nina both contracted malaria. All the construction material for the building and its entire contents – including a bath-tub from Marseilles – were carried out here by Corsican porters.

You should now see a cape jutting out a long way into the sea – **La Revellata**. Beyond it is **Calvi**, Genoa's first stronghold on the island and the one it kept for longest. Thanks to its airport and the many charter flights that arrive here, Calvi has developed into the most international of Corsica's resorts. There's a large selection of holiday bungalows, camp-sites and hotels.

13. Calvi

A morning stroll through the Citadel and the narrow streets beyond the quay. Lunch in the central square or down at the harbour. An afternoon excursion out into the Basse-Balagne.

I could spend hours in a wicker armchair outside a café on Calvi's Quai Landry, especially during the quiet months when the snow glistens high up on the massive Monte Grosso (1,938m/6,358ft)

opposite – but I know that the view of the bay and the mountains is far finer from up in the **Citadel**. So I suggest you follow my example and tear yourself away. Trot past the **Tour de Sel**, the salt-tower down beside the water, and walk up to the fortress above. Over the gateway to it you can read *Civitas semper fidelis* – Calvi was always loyal to Genoa.

From the first parapet, the cobblestones lead up and around to the **Place d'Armes**. On the left are the Sampiero barracks, formerly the governor's palace. On the other side of the street, a few steps beyond the row of facades, you can visit the **Oratoire de la Confrèrie Saint-Antoine** with its exhibitions of religious art (only open in peak season).

Citadel steps

Constructed according to a cruciform ground plan in the 13th century, and restored in the 18th century, the Church of **Saint-Jean-Baptiste** is surprisingly bright inside because of its lantern. On the left as you go in there are several old marble fonts, and if you carry on in a clockwise direction, you'll see a fine filigree tabernacle of dark wood in the first niche you come to, surrounded by some very ornate processional crosses. Go up a couple of steps, and inside a glass case there is a fine wooden madonna from Seville (1757) known as

The Citadel

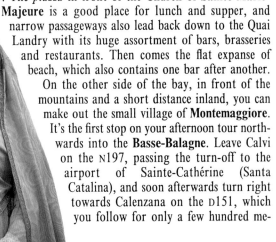

the **Virgin of the Rosary**. The figure is normally dressed in light blue, but during Easter week processions through the town, she wears black and, later, gold brocade.

The altar itself (16th century) is a masterpiece of intarsia work with polychrome marble. Behind it, among various busts of the clergy, is a triptych (1498) by the Ligurian artist Barbagelata. In the gap you can see the church's patron saint, John the Baptist, standing behind a group showing St Nicholas with children, probably carved locally. On the right of the altar stands a **Christ des Miracles**, which is said to have brought an end to the Turkish siege in 1553. In the direction of the entrance on both sides, above the richly-carved chancel, you can see the special boxes, with access from the outside, that were used by the town's wealthy families.

Flights of steps and various passageways lead past the church to the external fortifications. From the **Teghjale corner bastion** there's a superb view of both the bay and the Golfe de Revellata. In 1794, debris scattered by a shot fired from these very battlements struck Lord Nelson's right eye, destroying his sight; he had come ashore to assist with the capture of the town.

Down below, between the Boulevard Wilson and the Boulevard Clemenceau, you'll find all the holiday shopping you could possibly wish for. The *piazza* in front of the Church of **Sainte-Marie-Majeure** is a good place for lunch and supper, and narrow passageways also lead back down to the Quai Landry with its huge assortment of bars, brasseries and restaurants. Then comes the flat expanse of beach, which also contains one bar after another.

Virgin of the Rosary

On the other side of the bay, in front of the mountains and a short distance inland, you can make out the small village of **Montemaggiore**. It's the first stop on your afternoon tour northwards into the **Basse-Balagne**. Leave Calvi on the N197, passing the turn-off to the airport of Sainte-Cathérine (Santa Catalina), and soon afterwards turn right towards Calenzana on the D151, which you follow for only a few hundred metres before turning left on to the D451. Montemaggiore is beautifully situated on a rocky outcrop, and the church square offers a fine view of the gulf below. This village has a historic link with a man most people consider either a legend or an opera character – Don Juan. The family tree of an old-established local family proves that famous ladies' man Don Miguel de Leca y Colona y Magnara y Vincentello, born in Seville, Spain in 1627, actually had his family roots back here in Montemaggiore.

From the church square the D151 goes off to the left to Ile Rousse, and the view of Calvi and its bay from this road is the most breathtaking so far. The road finally reaches its highest point at the **Col de Salvi** (509m/1,670ft). At the crossroads in Cateri you then continue straight on and soon afterwards go up to the right, to **Sant'Antonino**. This village is just like an eagle's nest, perched on a ridge between two steep valleys, between the mountains and the sea. It dates back to the 9th century.

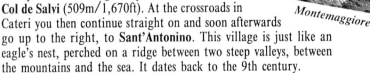

Montemaggiore

A good place to park is down on the left next to the church, and at this point don't be distracted by the flight of steps going straight up to the square, but instead walk off to the left and go up around the edge of the village. Of course you could be even more true to style, and hire a mule at the car park. Actually, all the typically wide and gently-sloping steps in these Corsican villages were built to accommodate the *pas d'âne* ('mule's pace'). Suddenly you'll find yourself in a *loghja*, or *corps de passage* – a series of vaulted passageways with lots of corners, leading to an enchanted little square with a chapel, before heading up to the highest houses

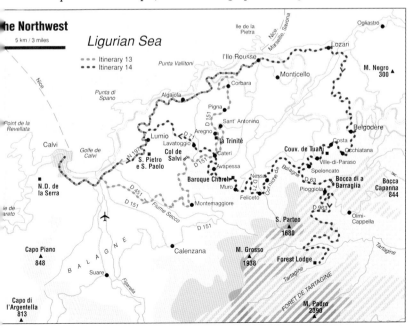

Detail of the Trinity Church

in the village. Fine view follows fine view, until the path finally takes you back to the church once again.

Rejoining the D151, turn sharp right and drive down in the direction of **Aregno**. Before you get there you pass the **Pisan Church of the Trinity** (1177) in its small graveyard, also consecrated to John the Baptist. Its warm, yellowish-brown stone forms a fine counterpart to the green-and-white of San Michele in Murato. The church has no tower, but take a close look at the figure below the gable: isn't it in the process of removing a thorn from its foot? The figure stands above four arches with varying types of decoration, supported by five animal statues. The two figures above the portal seem also to have been drawn directly from everyday life – a farmer and his wife, perhaps? Or a monk and a shepherd?

Pigna is the next village as you head closer towards the sea. Artistic traditions have been revived here ever since the 1960s: long-forgotten musical instruments have been recreated and old Renaissance songs are being rediscovered. Signposts point the way to the workshops and sales rooms of the **Corsicada**, and in the **Casa Musicale**, after dinner on the terrace, *lamentu* and *paghjella* (typical song-styles) are also served on Tuesday nights during peak season. You can also stay the night here or, if you prefer, in the monastery above the next village, **Corbara**.

From there it's just 5km (3 miles) to **Ile Rousse** (Isula Rossa), the town named after the red cliffs in its harbour. It was founded in 1758 by Pasquale Paoli in order to disrupt the supply route between Genoa and Calvi. Guarded ceremoniously by four palm trees, Paoli's bust gazes across a generously-proportioned square, situated right next to the beach. To end the day, how about a quick *pastis* outside my local, the **Café des Platanes**? The drive back to Calvi from here, via Algajola and Lumio, only takes around half an hour.

The Café des Platanes

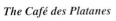

14. The Balagne

A whole row of ancient villages stretches across the Haute-Balagne like a string of pearls. Towering behind them are the northern peaks of the alpine massif. See map on page 59.

Following the route taken by the tour buses, you could see the Haute-Balagne in a morning or afternoon by travelling along its central *corniche*. But with so many villages and so many superb views it would be a shame not to visit the area beyond the mountain ridges, which is so mysterious that a whole day can go by in a flash. As with the previous day's excursion to the Basse-Balagne, leave Calvi in the direction of Bastia, but this time pass the turn-off to Calenzana and carry straight on past the Foreign Legion barracks.

The N197 takes you towards **Lumio** (Lumiu). Just before the village, on the right, you'll see the Chapel of **San Pietro e San**

Goats are bred for their milk

Paolo (turn right at the barrel with *'Vin'* written on it and park beside the cemetery). This 11th-century Pisan structure was probably built on the foundations of a Roman temple to Apollo or Mercury. The two enormous lion's heads carved in granite, guarding the portal, come from an earlier building.

Just after Lumio, turn half-right and follow signs to Lavatoggio and Belgodere on the D71. This is where the **Corniche de la Balagne** begins, the mountain road that passes through 10 villages and leads to five others, hugging the slopes and remaining at an altitude of around 300m (1,000ft) all the way.

Once you've passed the junction at Cateri, it's worth stopping at the next major bend in the road to admire the olive trees above the little village of **Avapessa**, some of which are nearly 1,000 years old. The mountain streams that flow continuously under the *corniche* here from November to May run into the Codole reservoir at the bottom of the valley, and there's a particularly attractive waterfall at the bridge beyond **Muro** (Muru) that has cut deep into the rock. The narrow main street of Muro is lined with arcades, and the massive baroque church contains a crucifix dating from 1659 that is supposed to possess miraculous powers. It failed to stop an accident in 1778, though, when the church roof fell in and killed 60 people. The village owed its former prosperity to the olive trade; the trees once used to fill the entire Regino valley.

Ville-di-Paraso

The same goes for **Feliceto** (Felicetu), which lies beneath the 1,700m (5,600ft) massif formed by San Parteo and Cima Caselle. Behind the church on the right, a glass-blower has a workshop *(verrerie)* and you can watch him at work on Monday, Wednesday and Friday. At the exit to the village, next to the bridge over the Regino, the millstones of the **Auberge U Mulinu** crush the olives every spring in time-honoured fashion to produce a fruity, high-quality oil – a technique that has mostly been superseded now by modern methods.

Nessa consists of just a handful of houses and a leafy square – it can be reached via a side-road which then leads back to the main road again. A short while later the D663 branches up to the right off the D71 in the direction of **Speloncato** (Speluncatu).

At a height of 550m (1,800ft) above sea-level, the road comes out into a square resembling an opera set. There's a fountain splashing away happily in the middle, where the inhabitants fill their mugs and plastic bottles with clear mountain spring water before mealtimes. Near a church, the **Hotel Spelunca** has set up quarters inside the former private palace of Cardinal Savelli, who served as secretary of state to Pope Pius until 1864. The cardinal's nickname, *il cane corso* ('the Corsican dog') betrays both the amount of influence he wielded and the amount of popularity he enjoyed. A few steps further on, the **Collegiate church** contains a real treasure: its organ (1810), which, despite having suffered a few 'practical' alterations over the years, has now been fully restored, and sounds superb. Concerts are held in San Michele between the end of June and the beginning of July – also as part of the *Festivoce* series (*see Calendar of Events*).

Both 'Speluncatu' and 'Spelunca' are derived from the Corsican word for the grottoes, *spelunce*, above which the town was built and which served formerly as sheep-pens or even as refuges from the Moors. Anyone who's worked up an appetite at this point can enjoy a simple snack at either of the two bistros in the square, while gazing out at everyday village life.

Between the U Fanale restaurant and the church, the D63 to Olmi Capella weaves its way up a bare mountain slope. After a few hairpins there's a good view of Speloncato below – and up at the top, at the **Bocca di a Battaglia** (1,099m/3,604ft), you have the entire Balagne at your feet. The view stretches from the Cap de la Revellata beyond Calvi, past the rocks off Ile Rousse with their lighthouses and the beaches at Lozari and Ostriconi, all the way to the Désert des Agriates near the Cap Corse.

If you turn to face the other side of the pass, you'll see Monte Padro (2,393m/7,850ft), the northern pillar of the alpine mountain range. Beneath this huge mountain, the road now descends into an almost completely green valley, so near and yet so far from the tourist world of the coast. Ancient, gnarled oak-trees cast their shade on the asphalt, and in **Pioggiola**, the first hamlet you come to, the **Auberge L'Aghjola** is a good place to stop and eat – as is the equally Corsican but rather inconspicuous **Auberge de la Tornadia** about half a mile further on. The menus here feature baby trout, fresh from the sparkling mountain streams at the foot of Monte Padro.

After lunch, take the road that bears off to the right in the direction of **Tartagine**. It's a pretty hair-raising route but beyond the bridge there's good parking to be had at Tartagine's dilapidated and absolutely beautiful forest lodge. You'll have to clamber either up or down river a bit here, but soon you'll find your very own rock-pool with its clear water, still refreshingly cool even at the very height of summer.

Suitably refreshed, you can now travel back the same way. At the square in Speloncato with its fountain, turn right down to **Ville-di-Paraso** (Parasu). Have a stroll through the vaulted passageways below the narrow main street and look at the restored parish church surrounded by pompous but dilapidated tomb-chapels. This is the type of scene which Maurice Utrillo and his mother Suzanne Valadon painted in the years leading up to World War I. Sadly, almost all of their paintings have disappeared from the area. At that time they lived in **Belgodère** (Belgudé), and on the way there you will pass through the idyllic villages of Costa and Occhiatana. The war memorial in Belgodère features the name 'Greco' – a relative of the singer Juliette Greco, who grew up here and began her career in Paris before becoming a famous celebrity.

The *corniche* of the Haute-Balagne stops here, and once you've passed the church, the journey back down to the coast takes around a quarter of an hour.

The coast at Lozari

Shopping

Corsica is officially a part of France, after all, so you don't only see the usual cheap holiday rags dangling in the vaulted cellars of the coastal towns – formerly used for storing wood – but also a great deal of *haute couture* straight from Paris. Alta Moda creations from neighbouring Milan are a lot more rare – one of the reasons why the Italian women who shop here tend to buy Parisian *chic*. For those in search of such attire, a leisurely look around the fashion shops here is definitely to be recommended.

A typical grocery

There's always a shop open somewhere, except on Sunday afternoons – and in holiday centres in peak season they stay open even then. Corsica's small village shops are actually open for a few hours every day of the week throughout the year – but they also tend to be on the expensive side because of having to mark up their goods to cover delivery costs. Such establishments are good for putting together a nice picnic lunch. You'll find home-grown tomatoes here, dark red and incredibly delicious, unlike the half-ripe variety the supermarkets down by the coast tend to stock. Or you might find a sausage smoked by your *epicière*'s brother-in-law that's a mouldy grey on the outside but very tasty on the inside. Keep an eye out for sweet biscuits, too, made according to local recipes. In fact the only thing you might find it hard to get hold of is bread, because the nearest baker sometimes lives a few villages away and a close count is thus kept on the loaves.

Island style, not always the height of fashion

65

Buy your herbs at the morning market

Markets

Every day except Sunday, from the crack of dawn, Ajaccio and Bastia have their morning markets at which you can buy fruit and veg, smoked meats, pastries, herbs and spices, cheese, honey, olive oil and wine. Fish is also sold in the neighbouring halls and shops. In the island's smaller villages you'll find the whole assortment among the pillars of a *marché couvert* (covered market). If the day's catch has been particularly good, the fishermen's wives often take up position outside the supermarkets with their baskets to sell their wares. At weekly markets – which irrationally tend to take place fortnightly – everyday clothing is sold, as are household goods for the local population, including cassettes of Corsican music (usually heard droning away very loudly in the background), junk, old postcards, and – in summer – jewellery and local crafts. The *forains* (market stallholders) travel from town to town. Other very local markets feature regional goods, and it's at these, as well as at the different regions' annual markets, that real bargains can be found.

Arts and Crafts

Even on an island with deeply-rooted craft traditions, there's quite a bit of kitsch around too, just as you'd expect. Of course if you don't mind, then a piece of horrid porcelain festooned with pictures of Napoleon might be just the souvenir for you. The island's serious artisans can usually be found in the shops bearing the names **Casa di L'Artigiani** or **Casa Paesana**. Here you will find a high-quality assortment of ceramics, baskets, Corsican woollen *(lana corsa)* pullovers and shawls, olive-wood carvings, baskets made from split chestnut branches or olive shoots, leather goods, painted silk, small sculptures and sketches, and even dried *macchia* in ceramic jars. Individual artisans, especially potters *(potiers)*, also signpost the way to their studios, which are often in remote villages and hard to find. Some studios proudly bear the **Corsicada** seal of quality – it originated in Pigna, a centre of traditional arts and crafts in the Lower Balagne, not far from Ile Rousse. *Diorit orbiculaire* is a form of dior-

The hallmark of quality

ite that can only be found in one private quarry on Corsica, and also in Finland. Small polished sections of this mineral with its interesting feldspar rings, also known as Corsite, can be bought at several souvenir shops on the island.

Antiques

The village houses belonging to old-established families are treasure-troves full of old, simply-made furniture and household objects, which are kept more for practical reasons than as status symbols. Typical are the *madia*, a trunk made of carved chestnut or lariciu pine, used to protect flour and bread from rats and field-mice, and the *bancu* (bench). You'll hardly ever see these marvellous old pieces of wooden furniture in the shops, though. Stores advertising *Brocante* or *Antiquitées* mostly contain wares from more recent times or other provinces, though some of them do stock decorative tools found in the barns of remote villages.

Souvenirs from the sea

Food and Drink

The earliest islanders were hunters, gatherers and collectors, and their expertise has been handed down through generations, thus guaranteeing the quality of Corsican meat, cheese and honey. The pigs here roam freely, and are more closely related to their wilder and hairier relatives than most. The veal and beef here doesn't contain any fast-growth hormones either. Nearly every village has its own secret recipe for ham *(prisuttu)*, lean steak *(lonzu)* or streaky bacon *(coppa)*. *Figatelli* is the name given to the strong-tasting mixture of liver-sausage and blood-sausage, toned down with herbs, which Corsicans love to roast over the fire and then eat with a slice of white bread. Wild boar, pigeon and starling pâtés are spiced with *nepita* (myrtle), a herb that tastes like a cross between mint and marjoram. Honey ranges from light to almost black, and the taste can be anything from light orange-blossom to dark and bitter-sweet *maquis*. Citrus fruits, kiwi, peaches, nuts, watermelons and blackberries are all used to flavour the island's different aperitif wines (most of them 15 percent alcohol), and the range of fruit and herb liqueurs is also huge.

People always used to say that the only wine Corsica produced was a very strong *vin ordinaire*. Most of the former cheap and high-yield vineyards have disappeared now, though, and Corsica's wine-makers are producing some fine-tasting wines from grapes suited to the sunny climate. The *Niellucciu* grape gives you a deep red wine with a strong bouquet; *Sciacarellu* is lighter and a lot fruitier; and the *Vermentinu* grape forms the basis for the island's dry whites. Each of the nine AOC regions also produces a fresh rosé. The naturally sweet *muscat* wines from the Cap Corse and Patrimonio are drunk as aperitifs and dessert wines right across the island.

Eating Out

Although foreign tourists have been bringing their own eating habits to the island for a few decades now, French and therefore Corsican restaurants have remained faithful to the old menu pattern of *hors d'oeuvres,* main dish, cheese and then dessert. There's sometimes another course too, and you'll usually be asked if you'd like an aperitif when you're handed the menu. All this might be all right for the evening, but for most tourists it's an expensive and time-consuming way of spending one's lunchtime – with the result that many seats in the restaurants remain empty. The ubiquitous *pizzeria* is one way out of the situation, but in the beach cafés, too, nobody will mind if you take a break between sunning yourself and surfing to order a mixed plate (*assiette mixte*), a colourful salad (*crudités*) or the dish of the day (*plat du jour*) with a drink.

Cuisine corse is simple, delicious and extremely filling – though in tourist areas it's not all that varied. The meal almost always starts with a selection of cold meats (*charcuterie*), followed by a minestrone-like *soupe corse* or a fish soup containing croutons and *rouille*, a delicious spicy mayonnaise with saffron and garlic. For the main course there's often *boeuf corse* or *sauté de veau*, beef or veal stew with olives and mushrooms, or lamb (*agneau*). Then there's

local sheep or goat's cheese varying from mild to strong, and to round off the meal, thinly-sliced apple cake, or cheesecake with a squeeze of lemon. This last dish, known as *fiadone* or, more rarely, *embrucciata*, contains one of the most delicious specialities: *brocciu*. Sheep or goat's milk is added to the whey after the cheesemaking process and rises to the surface when heated. The foam is then spooned off and placed into baskets, where it achieves cottage-cheese-like consistency. In desserts it is not only found in *fiadone* but in many other pastries, and sometimes it is eaten on its own with a dash of *eau-de-vie*. On the savoury side it is used in omelettes, and as a filling for canneloni and trout.

Café in Saint-Florent

Fresh Fish

The trout on Corsica either come straight from the island's mountain streams, or from fish-farms fed by mountain rivers. Salt-water fish only get caught by the local fishermen, unless strong winds prevent them from getting out in their tiny boats. Red mullet (*rouget*) or tuna-fish slices are grilled, but most typical of the island is the oven (*'au four'*) preparation of whole fish such as *chapon* (red weaver), *daurade* (gilthead) or *denti* (a type of perch), where the fish are baked on a bed of onions, tomatoes, fennel and herbs. *Denti* is also delicious when eaten cold with mayonnaise. There are no shrimps or prawns in Corsican waters, but lobster and spider-crab, *araignées*, squid (*calamares* and *seiches*) and octopus (*poulpes*) can all be found. On top of that, the mussels from the lagoons of Diane and Urbino on the east coast are fresh all year round. And in the cool season there are oysters too.

Marseilles is a Corsican bridgehead, and thus it's no wonder that the legendary *bouillabaisse* has also become part of the island's cuisine. The Corsicans call their version *aziminu*, and the compulsory ingredients include *rascasse* (a type of stickleback), *vive* (John Dory), *Saint-Pierre* and all manner of small crustaceans for the broth. It becomes *Royal,* and also particularly expensive, when rock-lobster gets added too. The odd bistro along the coast will also serve you *ormeaux* (stuffed mussels), and from the end of September sea-urchins (*oursins*), too, are eaten with wine and bread.

Age-old Recipes

The family-run restaurants in the mountain villages often have no written menu and you may sometimes find yourself being served with a dish that's been cooked according to an almost forgotten recipe, handed down orally from generation to generation. Instead of the usual assortment of cold meats, for instance, there's *misgiscia* – salted and smoked pieces of mutton and goat's meat. A very traditional main course is chestnut *pulenda* (polenta), roasted in slices with *cabri* (young kid) in a rich sauce. Or *sturzapreti*, spiced dumplings topped with baked cheese consisting of *brocciu*, spinach and eggs. In the wintertime you may also find wild boar *(sanglier)*, quail *(cailles)* or young partridge *(perdreaux)*. Then for pudding there's *pisticcine*, a small cake made from chestnut flour, or *migliacce*, a kind of *tortilla* made from *brocciu*.

Corsican Wines

The lowest wines in the French hierarchical list are *vins de pays* and *vins de table*, both of them clean and strong-tasting and served in a *pichet*, or clay jug. The next level up is VDQS (*Vin Délimité de Qualité Supérieure*), i.e. a good wine from a certain area. As far as the top classification, AOC (*Appelation d'Origine Contrôlée*), is con-

cerned, the state wine institute (known as INAO) controls the origin of the wine and sets a limit on the amount that can be produced per hectare in the respective region. A winemaker keen on quality will thus not only make sure he keeps his harvest below this limit, he will also press his grapes with the greatest possible care to produce the finest wine his soil can provide. Some vintners produce two AOC wines simultaneously. The *Clos Reginu* in the Balagne, for instance, which not only produces the fine wine of the same name but also an even better one – red, white and rosé – with the suffix *E Prove*. It was once the sole preserve of the priesthood. Top Corsican white wines include *Clos Nicrosi* from the Cap Corse, Orenga de Gaffory's *Blanc de Blancs* from Patrimonio, and the *Torraccia* from the region around Porto-Vecchio. Among the reds, the light wines of Patrimonio, the *Fiumicicoli* from Sartène and also *Clos Capitoro* and *Comte de Peraldi* from the Ajaccio area are particularly famous.

Restaurants

Mealtimes are just as sacred to the Corsicans as they are to the French. Lunch lasts from noon–2pm: before and after that time there is scarcely any restaurant service available anywhere. The beach establishments are an exception to the rule though, and so are the snack-bars, which will serve you *à toute heure* (around the clock) with a Corsican-style snack known as a *spuntinu*. Supper very rarely begins before 7.30pm – though it does get served slightly earlier during the tourist season – and the most crowded time of the evening is between 9pm and midnight, when the French and Italians, both used to eating late, squabble over the last few chairs. An aperitif is a good way of biding your time at this stage: a *Pastis* – the Corsican brand is called *Casanis* – or a *Cap Corse* which is made up from wine, herbs and quinine. Naturally, every waiter will be familiar with that French invention, the *kir* – white wine with a dash of blackcurrant liqueur – or the *Kir Royal*, the same thing with champagne instead of wine. Regular customers – and some *patrons* will treat you as one after only your second visit – are offered an *apéro*, or a *digestif* after the meal, free of charge.

Good cooks on Corsica tend to come and go – not surprisingly, really, when you consider that the restaurants here are only properly packed for four months in the year. Only very few of them succeed in maintaining their reputation year after year. The following list is a choice of establishments that you will find along the itineraries I have suggested. Unless otherwise stated, the price ranges apply to the cheapest menus without wine. The *à la carte* prices are considerably more expensive: *$* = 100–150FF; *$$* = 150–250FF; *$$$* = upwards of 300FF.

Bastia

AVEZZI
rue Saint Jean
Tel: 0495 310573
Pleasant balcony overlooking the Vieux Port. *$*

CASA CORSA
Quai des Martyrs de la Libération
Tel: 0495 310509
Seafood and Corsican specialities in a vaulted basement at the picturesque seafront between the new and old harbours. *$*

A CITADELLE
, rue du Dragon
Tel: 0495 314470
Situated in an alleyway opposite the Governor's Palace, this restaurant offers rustic, innovative cuisine featuring various local market produce. *$$*

Cap Corse
Nonza

AUBERGE PATRIZI
Tel: 0495 378216
A cosy restaurant on the village square, with Corsican menu. *$*

Centuri Port

LE VIEUX MOULIN
Tel: 0495 356015
A large terrace overlooking the fishing port. Features various game and seafood specialities, including *bouillabaisse*. *$-$$*

Nebbio
Saint-Florent

A RASCASSE
Tel: 0495 370699
Situated on the harbour front with a view over the bay from the first floor. Selected fish and shellfish creations. À la carte. *$$*

Dining at Calvi's Quai Landry

Muratu

AUBERGE DU MONASTERE
Tel: 0495 376418
Regional cuisine in the monastery annex of the parish church. *$*

Castagniccia
A Porta

CHEZ ELISABETH (L'Ampugnani)
Tel: 0495 392200
Behind the unassuming street facade is a terrace with mountain view. Two very reasonably priced menus in the Corsican tradition. *$* (wine included)

Piedicroce

LE REFUGE
Tel: 0495 358265
High above the valleys of the Castagniccia. Homemade specialities. *$*

Niolo/Corte
Pont de Castirla

CHEZ JACQUELINE
Tel: 0495 474204
Very popular Corsican menus include cheese *beignets*, *ragout* and *brocciu*, with brandy for desert. *$*

Corte

LA BOHEME
1, cours Pascal Paoli,
Tel: 0495 460923
Brasserie serving both local and classical dishes. *$*

Restonica Valley

AUBERGE DE LA RESTONICA
Tel: 0495 460958
Solid building at the entrance to the gorge, serving Corsican specialities from the stream and the forest. *$*

RELAIS DU LAC
Halfway up the valley road. Trout from the adjacent stream prepared in a variety of ways. *$*

The South
Cateraggio/Aleria

LE CHALET
Tel: 0495 570446
Situated on the Etang de Diane. Fish and seafood from the lagoon. *$*

Porto-Vecchio

GRAND HOTEL DE CALA ROSSA
Route de Cala Rossa
Tel: 0495 716151
Situated right on the bay, this is the best restaurant on the island. The finest fish, shellfish, lamb and venison are all prepared with great refinement. *$$–$$$*

Bonifacio

STELLA D'ORU/CHEZ JULES
3, rue St-Jean-Baptiste
Tel: 0495 730363
In an old house in the upper town. Exceptional regional cuisine. *$*

U CASTILLE
7 rue Simon-Varsi
Tel: 0495 730499
Wholesome Corsican food in the upper town. *$*

Sartène

AUBERGE SANTA BARBARA
Alzone, Route de Propriano
Tel: 0495 770906
Elaborate Corsican cuisine in seasona variation. A calm, rural place. *$$*

Tizzano

CHEZ ANTOINE
Tel: 0495 770725
Harbour bistro. Freshly caught fis and lobster. *$*

Ajaccio

LE POINT U
59, rue Fesch
Tel: 0495 215992
Superb regional cuisine in an 800 year-old vault. *$–$$*

L'ESTAMINET
6, rue du Roi-de-Rome
Tel: 0495 501042
Wine-bar in the old city. Excellen and wide choice of Corsican vintage brands, copious dishes. *$$*

After the summer crush

Relaxation at the harbour front

The West Coast
Sagone

L'ANCURA
Tel: 0495 280493
One terrace faces the sea and the other the mountains. The cuisine comes from both. *$*

Cargèse

BEL MARE
Tel: 0495 264013
At the entrance to the village, this restaurant offers simple but good cuisine high above the bay. *$*

Porto

LE ROMANTIQUE
Tel: 0495 261085
Situated at the marina, it has a small terrace overlooking the sea. Good basic cuisine. *$*

Calvi

SANTA MARIA
Place de L'Eglise
Tel: 0495 650419
Like a stage in front of the church steps. A large selection of food. *$*

LA VILLA
Chemin de Notre-Dame-de-la-Sierra
Tel: 0495 651010
One of the best restaurants on the island, situated in a 4-star hotel above the town. Delicious gourmet creations. *A la carte* only. *$$$*

CAPUCCINO
Quai Landry
Tel: 0495 651119
Under a sun roof opposite the harbour entrance, specialises in pasta dishes. *$*

The Balagne
Pioggiola

AUBERGE DE LA TORNADIA
Tel: 0495 619093
Popular country restaurant. Several comprehensive Corsican menus. *$*

Ile Rousse

U SPUNTINU
1, rue Napoléon
Tel: 0495 600005
A few paces from the Place Paoli in the Old Town. Interesting meat and fish menus; excellent wines. *$*

Calendar of Special Events

There's no folk-dancing to be seen on Corsica any more. Centuries of oppression and suffering have removed it, along with the colourful costumes that one still sees on old etchings and postcards. A black dress for elderly ladies, and here and there a red sash with a corduroy jacket for men, might still just qualify as folkwear.

In contrast, another nearly extinct tradition has been revived in recent years: vocal polyphony, a musical form that had its heyday in the 16th century. It is an archaic form of singing whereby three basic voice-lines, known as *a secunda*, *u boldu* (or *u bassu*) and *a terza* blend together, each one relatively autonomous and reaching its own climaxes. This intense harmony is supposed to produce a so-called 'angel's voice', a line above the other three, which doesn't actually exist.

As recently as the 1980s anyone who wanted to hear this form of singing had to make the pilgrimage to various remote villages on religious festival days. There they would hear a handful of elderly local shepherds singing mass in the form of a *paghjella*. A *paghjella* invests even profane texts with a near-religious character, and is the island's common property, passed down through generations in verse form (usually two octameters). It is never written down, but kept alive in melodic form, and often differs from valley to valley.

It is not only the politically-active male voice choirs eager to stress their 'corsitude' who add the *paghjella* to their repertoire: mixed and female groups have raised this form of unaccompanied singing to the status of an art-form. Singers have now introduced it to the world at large: the Nouvelles Polyphonies Corses could be heard at the opening ceremony of the 1992 Winter Olympics at Albertville. Today it's no longer difficult to gain access to genuine Corsican musical tradition. An evening listening to a *paghjella* and also to simple monodic singing, such as the old *lamentu* (lament), must certainly number among the most vivid memories of a holiday on the island.

RELIGIOUS FESTIVALS

The religious year begins with **Epiphany** on 6 January. Special cakes can be bought at the local *boulangerie* or in the supermarket, into which a *fève* – either a large dried bean or a plastic symbol – has been baked. Whoever finds it in his piece of cake becomes the 'king' and is allowed to wear a golden paper crown. **Carni-**

Easter Procession

val, unlike the event in neighbouring Nice, is not a last chance for revelry before Lent, but is almost exclusively a children's festival and is sometimes even celebrated after Easter, as local timetables dictate.

As in other Mediterranean countries, **Easter Week** is of great importance. A series of sometimes quite dramatic acts of faith begins on **Palm Sunday**, or *palmiers*. Artistically plaited palm-tree leaves are brought into the church to be blessed, and are supposed to bring a whole year's peace to their households. Processional figures are removed from their various niches in the churches, and dressed in religious finery. Worshippers place lighted candles at their feet.

On **Good Friday** the male members of the religious fraternities, known as *confrèries*, carry the processional figures (which are enormously heavy and are sometimes in groups known as *chasses*) through the crowds of worshippers. In some towns – with particular fervour practised in Calvi – the procession of *confrèries* becomes a *granitula* or *girandula*, a kind of spiral that keeps forming and re-forming, like an archaic symbol of man's existence from embryo to death and then to rebirth.

Erbalunga at Cap Corse is renowned for its circular variation, known as *cerca*. In Bonifacio the itineraries of several *confrèries* cross at different times during the day, and in Corte a *Christ mort* gets carried through the streets at dusk. In Sartène thousands of people line the streets to watch a penitent known as the *catenacciu*, wrapped in a red cowl, shouldering a wooden cross and dragging a heavy chain, *a catena*, attached to his ankle. More and more towns on the island seem to be adopting this tradition – all that sunshine seems to produce quite a few 'sinners' these days.

The second major festival in the church year – apart from Ascension – is the **Immaculate Conception** on 8 September. The statues of the Virgin are removed from the churches once again, and there is a particularly famous procession in the Niolo village of Casamaccioli (*see Itinerary 5*). There's also a very colourful fair held there, which is known as **A Santa** for short. On **All Saints' Day** *(Toussaint)*, candles and huge chrysanthemum bushes are carried to the graveyards.

At **Advent** the churches start filling up with cribs, and in Bastia there's actually an **international crib show**. The continental habit of placing a Christmas tree in one's drawing-room is still not all that widespread on Corsica – though the supermarkets shower you for weeks on end with Bing Crosby, Ella Fitzgerald and various choirs. It's at Christmas time that the shelves in the shops here start to bend under the sheer weight of French specialities that the Corsicans usually have to do without. The highlight of **Christmas Eve** is the traditional *bûche*.

t's actually the broadest part of a tree-trunk, which the menfolk saw down to size and which is then meant to crackle away in an open fireplace until everyone gets back from mass – but the *bûche* you find today is made of pastry, covered with various bits of decoration, and usually contains a sickly-sweet filling.

The big Christmas meal and the exchanging of presents take place on the **first day of Christmas** – there isn't a second one, the shops are already open again by then, just as they are late into Christmas Eve. **New Year's Eve** is the time for parties and balls, enlivened not only with fireworks and blanks but often with real ammunition too.

SECULAR FESTIVALS

On the evenings of Midsummer, **Saint-Jean**, and the French national holiday on **14 July** you will come across firework displays in the resort towns. On a date around July 20 Bastia commemorates the succession (rotation) of the Genoese governor in an historical setting. In Ajaccio, Napoléon's birthday (15 August 1769) is very noisily celebrated.

The summer festivals begin with a lively **jazz festival** in Calvi in June. Immediately after it, and also in the Balagne, there is the **Festivoce**, a concert series in which local artists get together with performers from abroad. That's when the restored organs in the villages up in the mountains resound once more, when polyphonic harmonies are heard, and when *chiam'e rispondi*, a kind of mock-poetic question-and-answer game, gets recited off the cuff. In brief, the island's recently regained cultural self-confidence gets into its stride.

Other highlights are the **Rencontres Polyphoniques** at the end of

September in Calvi, a **Classical Music Festival** in early September in Bonifacio, and the **Mediterranean Culture Film Festival** in Bastia, held in the last two weeks of October. In the same month Calvi, almost deserted by the tourists so late in the year, stages its **Wind Festival**, and there's certainly enough wind around that late in the year. Kites fly high above the beach, hang-gliders hover above the slopes, scientists give lectures, and every evening musical performances are greeted by stormy applause.

Alongside many other events – in summer the newspapers have page after page of information – the **Tour de Corse** is an established part of the annual calendar: at the beginning of May, rally drivers from several different countries roar their way around the twisting and narrow mountain roads between Ajaccio, Corte, Bastia and Calvi.

Rather more sedate are the sailing regattas held between the Côte d'Azur and Calvi, which use the island of Giraglia, with its lighthouse, as a turning-point.

Veteran sings his piece

PRACTICAL information

The ferry arrives

GETTING THERE

By Air

Air France operate direct scheduled flights from Paris and Lyon to Ajaccio (Campo dell'Oro Airport), from Paris to Bastia (Poretta Airport) and Calvi (Sainte Cathérine/Santa Catalina Airport). More irregular but much less expensive connections are offered by Nouvelles Frontières. Air Littoral has flights from Bordeaux to Ajaccio and Bastia. The Compagnie Corse Méditerranée has regular connections from Marseille and Nice. If you're flying from the UK both British Airways and Air France operate daily scheduled flights from London Heathrow to Nice or Marseille. From there the Compagnie Corse Méditerranée (CCM, bookings through Air France /Air Inter) will carry you on to the aforementioned island airports. Both British Airways and Air France operate daily scheduled flights from London Heathrow to Ajaccio via Nice or Marseille. The onward flight will be with Compagnie Corse Méditerranée. Charter airlines offer direct flights from London and Manchester as well as from several cities in France and Western Europe to Ajaccio, Bastia or Calvi. There are also charter flights to Figari near Porto Vecchio. Departures from the UK are generally from Gatwick; TAT operates a service from Stansted to Calvi and Figari.

From the airports in Ajaccio and Bastia there are buses to take you to the city centres. In Calvi there are taxis.

By Sea

Ferries between the French mainland and Corsica, operated by SNCM, are available the whole year round from Marseille and Nice to Ajaccio and Bastia, and also at least once a week from Nice to Ile Rousse. During peak season there are also connections from Toulon on the mainland, and Calvi, Propriano and Ile Rousse all get visited. From April to October there are speedboats (NGV = Navires à Grande Vitesse) from both SNCM and Corsica Ferries operating between Nice and Ajaccio, Bastia, Ile Rousse and Calvi. For visitors departing from Italy, Corsica Ferries ply regularly between Livorno and Bastia, and during peak season there are also connections from Savona to Bastia and Ile Rousse.

The right footwear is important

MOBY lines departs from Genoa, Livorno and Piombino to Bastia, and offer through-tickets via Bonifacio to Santa Teresa-di-Gallura on the island of Sardinia. Corsica Marittima runs a number of boats from Genoa and Livorno to Bastia. There are also ferries operating between Santa Teresa-di-Galliura (on the island of Sardinia) and Bonifacio.

All ports of departure in France and Italy can be reached directly via motorway. As an alternative to driving your own car to the ferry terminal there are several SNCF motor-rail services that you might want to consider, not only those departing from Paris, but also the direct overnight connections between Calais and Nice, Boulogne and Livorno.

TRAVEL ESSENTIALS

When to Visit

The coastal resorts are packed from mid-July until the end of August. Visiting the island during these weeks can prove pretty tiresome, especially because it's so hot. The ideal time to travel would be from the end of May onwards, and then again after the first week in September. Before the peak holiday season the island is still green, and covered with flowers that fill the air with that incomparable scent which made Napoleon once say that he could recognise his native island anytime with his eyes closed. Until mid-May the climate is usually unpredictable, and from the beginning of October onwards there are quite a few showers. There again, the weather tends to stabilise nicely in November, and then stays mostly fine until Christmas. In January and February snow often falls as low as the 300m (1,000ft) mark. High mountain passes can suddenly be closed by snowfalls as late as May.

Visas and Passports

Citizens of EU countries, Andorra, Austria, Cyprus, Finland, Iceland, Liechtenstein, Malta, Monaco, Norway, Sweden, Switzerland, Canada and the US do not need a visa to visit France. All other nationals should get in touch with the visa section of their local French embassy or consulate before travelling.

Clothing and Luggage

Remember if you're travelling round the island that temperatures can get extremely 'alpine' in the mountain villages. If you go hiking, even close to the coast, you'll need shoes with good grip because the paths are stony and there's quite a bit of loose rock about. Wearing a hat or headscarf as well as a strong sun-cream with a high protection factor is absolutely vital for those planning any kind of mountain tour, even in the cooler months. It is best not to brave the *macchia* in shorts as most of the smaller shrubs in this vegetation zone are thorny. Decent clothes are an absolute must for any church visit if you don't want to offend local sensibilities, and in the remote villages you'll find that scanty clothing is also widely disapproved of.

Electricity

The electrical current in Corsica is 220 volts. When using rather sensitive electrical appliances (such as radios, video cameras, etc.) bear in mind that the voltage is not as stable as it is on the mainland. Variations anywhere between 190 and 250 volts are quite possible. Don't forget to take an adaptor for any appliance you bring from home.

Time Zone

For most of the year, France is one hour ahead of Greenwich Mean Time; if it is noon in Nice, it is 11am in London, 5am in New York and Toronto and 8pm in Melbourne.

GETTING ACQUAINTED

Geography

With an area of 8,800 sq km (3,352 sq miles), Corsica is the fourth largest island in the Mediterranean, after Sicily, Sar-

Sculpture at Ile Rousse promenade

Government and Economy

Corsica belongs to France and, as has always been the case, French politics are decided upon in Paris. Corsican inhabitants have always felt that this is something of an affront and since the 1960s a regional movement has been increasingly involved in combating this particular situation. In 1975 Corsica's administration was divided into two *départements*: the Corse du Sud (Ajaccio Prefecture) and the Haute-Corse (Bastia Prefecture). Taken together these two *départements* make up the Region Corse (with its headquarters located in Ajaccio), which has been given a certain amount of authority in making governmental decisions. In 1982 Corsica received a statute of autonomy, granting it – in theory – extensive authority. In the wake of the outbreaks of violence and strikes in 1991 and subsequent elections in 1992, another even more extensive statute has been granted. But this certainly won't be the last step: for many Corsicans autonomy is not the same as independence.

A good third of the gainfully employed population in Corsica is occupied in some sort of agricultural pursuit. Particularly in the east, there are large orchards of apples, cherries and plums. Large-scale irrigation has enabled the cultivation of citrus fruits. Olives and chestnuts are cultivated for local consumption. In the area around Porto Vecchio, cork production

dinia and Cyprus. The island is 183km (115 miles) long from Cap Corse in the north to Capo Pertusato in the south. At its widest point it measures 83km (52 miles). The coastline measures 1,000km (625 miles). The island is basically a mountain range jutting out of the sea. With the exception of the coastal plains in the east, it is characterised by steep hills and mountains. Monte Cinto at 2,710m (8,891ft) is the highest peak.

Population

Corsica has a population of about 250,000, of whom over 40 percent reside in the two principal towns of Ajaccio and Bastia. Members of old-established Corsican families, who have lived on the island for centuries, still make up the majority of the residents, despite the emigrations. Ever since the Genoese first arrived, many young Corsicans have chosen to go to the mainland. Corsica also has a tradition of immigration: in addition to the Greek Orthodox refugees who finally settled in Cargèse after much turmoil, nowadays there are Moroccans who come to Corsica as agricultural and construction workers. The immigrant population was also bolstered by the settlement of 17,000 Algerian-French between 1962 and 1966.

The Moor with his headband

is also significant. High-quality wines are produced on Cap Corse (Rogliano), in the Nebbio (Patrimonio) and in the areas around Ajaccio, Sartène and Figari.

The most important source of revenue is tourism. A large portion of tourist-related businesses are operated by French people from the mainland or Algerian-French. With the exception of a few medium-sized businesses in Ajaccio and Bastia there is scarcely any industry to speak of. Coastal fishing does not contribute markedly to the economy.

Religion

The native population is almost without exception Roman Catholic. But only the women are regular church-goers; the men only enter the church during festivals. There is Sunday mass in the main towns, otherwise services are very irregular, administered by itinerant priests on certain days of the week.

MONEY MATTERS

The currency on Corsica is the French franc. Eurocheques are accepted at banks; the highest amount you can cash is 1,400FF, and the cheque needs to be made out to the bank. There's a good exchange rate for traveller's cheques; if you exchange cash, though, you tend to lose out. Banks are open mornings and afternoons, except at weekends. Foreign currency exchange establishments stay open longer but often take much higher commissions or give you a less favourable rate than the main banks. Eurocard, Visa and American Express are the most commonly accepted credit cards; you can use them in all major hotels, restaurants, and also at service stations. There are cash dispensers outside most banks and major post offices.

Tipping

Most bills, when you get them, are presented in *servis compris* form, i.e. the tip is included. It's customary, though, to leave your waiter or waitress a tip of 10 percent or so, and taxi-drivers, too, expect you to round up the figure.

GETTING AROUND

By Car

Driving along the usually narrow, often confusing and badly-surfaced roads is tiring and often dangerous. Corsicans tend to drive fast, without a care in the world – all those dents in their cars, and the various wrecked cars at the bottom of the island's ravines are proof enough. Don't hesitate to sound your horn loudly and regularly whenever you encounter a blind corner – mind you, it won't have any effect on cows or donkeys, who often choose just such places to graze. Fallen rock tends to remain where it is for ages, or it gets painted orange to warn drivers. Orange plastic tape is also used to warn drivers of other surprise hazards. Deep puddles in the road after heavy rain can also often force you to drive in the other lane. Don't expect to travel any faster than an average speed of 30 to 40 kph (around 20 mph) along the island's narrow twisting roads.

You may be surprised at the various ways of spelling place-names on maps and road-signs. More and more parishes on the island are remembering their Corsican names, but no overall concept has been formulated as yet. The Italian suffix -*o* has been turned into a -*u* by the nationalists with a dot of white paint; several mayors place both versions above each other; others surprise everyone by using names that can't be found on any maps at all. Some place-name signs have been rendered completely illegible by nationalist graffiti or have simply been painted over altogether. I have taken account of this recent development in the itinerary descriptions.

The marina in Propriano

There are hire cars available at all the island's airports, towns and larger tourist centres. It's usually a good idea to order a car in advance from home and pay for it there – the rates are cheaper that way. However there are also cheap local rates available *(forfaits)*. Whatever you decide to do, it is highly advisable to take out a comprehensive insurance on the car *(franchise)*.

By Train

Bastia, Calvi and Ile Rousse are connected to Corte and Ajaccio via a narrow-gauge diesel railway line. The Corsicans refer to it as *u trinichellu* ('the little railway') and the French as *la Micheline*. There are two connections daily in each direction; the trip from Bastia to Calvi takes 3 hours and 15 minutes, and the one to Ajaccio around 4 hours. The Calvi-Ile Rousse route operates more frequently from the end of June to the end of September and stops at the beaches if required. The trip across the alpine watershed from Ponte Leccia to Ajaccio, is a real experience.

The Bastia–Biguglia route on the east coast, and the Calvi–Ile Rousse one on

'La Micheline' at the station

the west coast are used more frequently because they are tramways. A real experience is the trip across the alpine watershed, from the junction at Ponte Leccia to Ajaccio.

By Bus

There are bus connections throughout the year between Bastia, Ponte Leccia, Corte and Ajaccio, Bastia and Porto-Vecchio, Bastia and Ile Rousse/Calvi and Ajaccio, Cargèse, Porto, and – in peak season – between Saint-Florent and Ile Rousse/Calvi. Bus excursions are offered from all holiday centres in Corsica.

Visitors who come to the island without their cars can discover some of the most beautiful scenery in Corsica by joining up with one or more of these relatively inexpensive bus tours.

By Bicycle and Boat

Cyclists can experience the varied landscape and vegetation contained in a small area more intensely than car passengers. Traffic is especially minimal along minor roads in the island's interior. A good map is indispensable for bike touring. It's also possible to rent bicycles in Corsica, particularly in the coastal resorts.

For those visitors wishing to get to know Corsica by boat, but who do not own their own ocean-going vessel, tour agencies offer a number of opportunities in the form of organised cruises or yacht voyages.

Boat excursions present an enjoyable and relatively inexpensive means by which to explore the Corsican coastline. All the following trips are possible: Ajaccio to the Iles Sanguinaires; Bonifacio to the Grotte du Sdragonato and other caves in the sea cliffs as well as to the islands of Lavezzi, Baïnzo and Cavallo; Calvi to Girolata; Saint-Florent to beaches in the Agriates region; and from Porto to the Calanche of Piana.

Maps

A detailed pull-out map is included in the back of this guide. Corsica is also covered by the maps Carte Michelin 90, 1:200 000 and Carte IGN (*Institut Géographique National*) 116 Série Rouge 1:250 000.

The island is covered in two halves, at a scale of 1:100 000 by the IGN Série Verte maps 73 (north) and 74 (south).

For more detailed coverage showing paths etc, the IGN TOP maps on a scale of 1:25 000 are recommended.

HOURS & HOLIDAYS

Opening Hours

Most shops open their doors between 9am and 10am in the morning, and bakeries open as early as 7am. They then take a lunch-break from noon till 3pm before finally closing at around 7pm. Variations of half an hour or so each way are quite common. These times apply all year round and include Saturday. In the peak season, supermarkets are open all day and often on Sunday mornings as well.

Public Holidays

Public holidays on Corsica are 1 January, Easter Sunday, Easter Monday, 1 May, 8 May (1945 Armistice Day), Ascension Day, Whit Monday, 14 July, 8 September (Assumption of the Virgin Mary), All Saints' Day, 11 November (1918 Armistice Day), and Christmas Day. Though most offices and shops always close on these days, you will usually be able to find the odd baker or village shop remaining open. If public holidays happen to fall on a Thursday or Tuesday, banks and government departments 'bridge the gap' *(faire le pont)* by interposing an extra day off either before or after the relevant weekend.

ACCOMMODATION

From early July until the end of August, accommodation on the island is extremely hard to find unless you've reserved in advance – even in the mountain villages. The best time to book for this period is around Easter or even before.

The off-season

The local tourist information offices (Syndicats d'Initiative or Offices de Tourisme) keep useful lists of hotels and rental accommodation. To find out the prices you often have to go directly to the respective hotel or landlord.

Hotels

There are over 400 hotels on Corsica, most of them on the coast. The majority are 2-star. In the island's interior you'll often find rather basic 1-star establishments. If you reserve in advance, expect to be asked to make a deposit (*arrhes*). The following is a selection of recommended hotels in and around the major centres covered in this guide:

$ = 250–450FF
$$ = 350–750FF
$$$ = 500–900FF
$$$$ = more than 900FF

Bastia

POSTA VECCHIA
Quai des Martyres de la Libération
Tel: 0495 323238
Situated on the edge of the Old Town. Mostly small rooms, but some of them enjoy a sea view. *$*

Pietranera/Palagaccio

L'ALIVI
Route du Cap (3km north of Bastia)
Tel: 0495 316185
All the rooms in this long building have balconies above the cliffs. *$$*

Etang de Biguglia

ISOLA HOTEL
Lido de la Marana (13km south of Bastia)
Tel: 0495 331960
On the semi-circular bay between the beach and the lagoon. *$–$$*

Niolo and the Bozio

DOMINIQUE COLONNA
Vallée de la Restonica
Tel: 0495 610545
On the river at the start of the gorge. $

Bustanico

HOTEL U LICCEDU
Tel: 0495 486623
Friendly local hotel in the Bozio village of Bustanico. $

The South
Bonifacio

GENOVESE
Haute Ville
Tel: 0495 731234
Luxurious, converted Genoese mansion high above the fjord. $$$$

LE ROYAL
Rue Fred Scamaroni
Tel: 0495 730051
Simple but comfortable hotel in the upper town, with a view of the fjord. $

LE ROY D'ARAGON
13, Quai Comparetti
Tel: 0495 730399
Stylishly renovated old hostel between the port and the cliffs. $$$

Sartène

VILLA PIANA
Route de Propriano
Tel: 0495 770704
Built in terraces with view of the sea and the mountains. $

Propriano

GRAND HOTEL MIRAMAR
Route de la Corniche
Tel: 0495 760313
Modern, overlooking the gulf. $$

The West Coast
Ajaccio

ALBION
15, Avenue Général Leclerc
Tel: 0495 216670
Classical building near the Place d'Austerlitz. $$

FESCH
7, Rue Fesch
Tel: 0495 216262
Traditional Corsican hotel right in the heart of the old town. $–$$

HOTEL DU GOLFE
5, Boulevard du Roi Jérôme
Tel: 0495 214764
Opposite the docks with a view of the market and sea. $–$$

Porto

LES FLOTS BLEUS
Marina
Tel: 0495 261126
Balcony rooms with view of the tower and the bay. $

Calvi

BALANEA
6, rue Clemenceau
Tel: 0495 659494
On the harbour with an extensive view of the Gulf and the mountains. $$$–$$$$

SAINT-ERASME
Route d'Ajaccio
Tel: 0495 650450
On the coast road between the Citadel and Cap Revellata. $$

LE MAGNOLIA
Place du Marché
Tel: 0495 651916
Very comfortable, with a garden courtyard, tranquillity in the town centre. $$$

Rental Apartments

Villas and apartments are advertised in the papers at home. Otherwise they can be booked through the local tourist offices. Other options are *gîtes ruraux*, bungalows and private rooms (*chambres d'hôtes*).

Le Magnolia in Calvi

Camping

Corsica's wild, rugged scenery makes you want to pitch your tent anywhere you like – you're not allowed to, though, because of the danger of fire and other environmental damage. The choice of proper camp-sites, however, is huge. Some are close to villages, others high in the mountains. Even during peak season there's always room.

HEALTH & EMERGENCIES

Reciprocal agreements regarding medical protection exist between the different European Union countries. But even EU visitors may want to take out additional cover. Visitors from outside the EU should certainly make sure they have medical insurance. Most doctors in Corsica can speak at least a little English. The SAMU *(Service d'Aide Médicale Urgente)* is on hand in case of emergencies.

There are fully-equipped hospitals in Ajaccio and Bastia, another near Porto-Vecchio, and in Calvi an *Antenne médicale* is on hand to deal with less serious cases.

The addresses of chemists open for emergency service nights and weekends *(Pharmacie d'urgence)* are posted in chemist shop windows. There are chemists in both Ajaccio and Bastia that remain open until 8pm during the summer tourist season.

Emergency Numbers

Emergency medical aid (& ambulance): 15
Police: 17
Fire Brigade: 18
Sea Rescue: 0495 201363

Emergency medical service can also be reached by calling the following numbers:
Ajaccio: SAMU. Tel: 0495 215050
Bastia: Centre Hospitalier Paese Nuovo. Tel: 0495 331515
Centre Hospitalier Général Falconaja. Tel: 0495 303030
Calvi: SAMU Antenne Médicale . Tel: 0495 651122
Corte: Hôpital Civil. Tel: 0495 450500
Porto Vecchio: SAMU. Tel: 0495 770005
Sartène: Hôpital Cacciabello. Tel: 0495 779500

Security and Crime

In the towns pick-pockets and purse-snatchers are at work and theft also occurs in more rural areas as well as on nearly empty beaches. Car thieves, who usually frequent the larger towns and coastal resorts, are quick and efficient.

Terrorism and Strikes

Visitors should not be alarmed by reports of terrorism. Attacks by heavily-disguised commando squads on more or less illegally-built housing or against objects of speculation built at the islanders' expense tend to be limited to the winter season, when the buildings are standing empty. In late summer, however, forest fires can pose a threat to campsites. The strikes by French ferry and aircraft operators can also be unpleasant – they tend to take place unannounced in the period before peak season.

COMMUNICATIONS & NEWS

Post

Post offices *(Bureau de Poste)* in Corsica are open from 8am–noon and 3–6pm. The hours at smaller branch offices *(Agence Postale)* vary. Postcards and letters weighing up to 20 grams destined for other European Community countries are considered as domestic mail in terms of postage (3FF). Stamps may be purchased in the *Bureaux de Tabac* as well as from post offices.

Telephone

All French telephone numbers have ten digits starting with 0. For telephone connections within France it isn't necessary to first dial a dialling code. Calls placed to Paris from Corsica must be prefaced by dialling 16-1.

To call Corsica from a foreign country dial 33 for France and 495 for Corsica, followed by the remaining six digits. There are less and less telephone boxes in France and Corsica which accept coins (50 centimes, 1, 2 or 5 francs), but there are telephones in bars and other public places which do under the sign of 'Point Phone'. Most of the telephone kiosks now have card phones; Telecards can be purchased in post offices and tobacco shops. To call other countries, first dial the international access code 00: Australia (61); Germany (49); Italy (39); UK (44); US and Canada (1). If using a US credit phone card, call the company's access number below: AT&T, Tel: 11-0010; MCI, Tel: 078 11-0012; Sprint, Tel: 078 11-0014.

The Media

There are two daily newspapers which appear in Corsica: the *Corse Matin* and *La Corse*. Both are the Corsican editions of newspapers published on the French mainland (*Nice Matin* and *Le Provençal*, respectively) and contain and contain several pages of regional and local information. In contrast to these are purely Corsican-nationalist magazines with some of their articles appearing in Corsican.

For most of the year, foreign magazines and newspapers are only available in the main towns and tourist centres but in summer you can find them in al most every *Maison de la Presse*.

The six French television networks ar in part privately and in part publicly op erated. FR3 is a regional programme fo Corsica. On the east coast Italian televi sion stations can frequently be received Now that satellite TV has been introduced international reception is extremely good

NIGHTLIFE

The nightlife in the coastal resorts is vi brant, although the discos are only really packed during the three summer months In May, and in September too, these es tablishments – some of which are abso lutely huge – are yawningly empty and extremely tedious. During the rest of the year they only open their doors at week ends, or for the odd special occasion.

In season, things only begin to hot up quite late, usually around midnight, and then the fun lasts right through till dawn. The entry price (60FF on average) usu ally includes your first drink – all the others after that cost a lot more. Some times posters promise some attraction or other, and dancing takes second place. There may be an erotic lingerie fashion show at the beginning of the season – that's when the qualifying rounds for 'Miss Corsica' are held in all the coastal towns. Things really get going, though, once the

West Coast sunset

young Italians are over for the summer. Almost every holiday centre has its 'Miss Italia'. As the summer suntans start to get darker there's never any shortage of candidates for these contests. But even beach-bars which at lunchtimes are normally quiet, upright-looking establishments become transformed once evening comes around. Cocktails are served instead of salads, and quite often you'll see the odd steamy Brazilian female singer writhing away to the sound of a combo.

The so-called cabarets provide late-evening performances of good, old-fashioned folklore. Not a synthesizer in sight – here the performers plonk a stool under their leg to support the guitar and then deliver a whole series of nostalgic melodies, of the type Tino Rossi used to captivate Parisians with in the 1930s.

Finally, in July and August there are village fêtes held in central squares, where prices are very reasonable and visitors are welcome. Elderly couples can waltz and tango to their heart's content at these kind of functions, and even pop and disco-sounds have now made their entry on local scenes. But young people mostly find what they're looking for during their tourism apprenticeship down on the coast. Perhaps these hinterland evenings are the most Corsican of all, though: under the trees with their garlands of lights, hearing the owls hoot on your way home, and seeing an illuminated church-tower that stays in your memory for years afterwards.

USEFUL INFORMATION
Flora and Fauna

In the *Parc Naturel Régional de la Corse*, which covers the whole of the central mountain chain as well as the Castagnic-cia, there are still moufflons (a type of wild sheep), eagles and bearded vultures to be found, and in the Scandola maritime reserve several very rare species of bird, including ospreys, can still be seen flying around. Falcons and sparrowhawks circle above even the lowest of the mountain villages, and further up there are also goshawks and buzzards. The *macchia* contains wild boar, quail and partridge. There are no poisonous snakes on Corsica, though perhaps the odd miniature scorpion. The sheer amount of different species of butterfly is stunning. Orchids grow everywhere, including the roadside; 300m (980ft) up, tiny cyclamen can be seen; even higher up you'll find white amaryllis. In the shallows of quiet bays you might be unlucky enough to tread on the poisonous dorsal fin of a *vive* (John Dory) that has settled into the sand, and the spikes on the sea-urchins are almost as painful: they lurk just below the waterline on rocks.

Museums

The opening times of museums vary. Almost all of them are open in the morning 9am–noon, and then again in the afternoon 2–6pm. Some close on Sundays or for a few weeks in the winter. Museum admission is usually around 10FF; only a few are more expensive.

Ajaccio

CHAPELLE IMPÉRIALE
The mausoleum of the imperial family, built in 1857 during Napoleon III's reign.
MUSÉE FESCH
In the main section between the chapel and the library. Italian masters dating from the 14th to 18th century.
BIBLIOTHEQUE FESCH
Also open on Friday evenings in the summer. In the left wing of the Palais Fesch. Impressive collection of old books. Founded by Napoleon's brother Lucien: as interior minister, he confiscated the books from monasteries and stately homes. Several fine exhibits.
MAISON NATALE DE NAPOLEON
One of France's national museums. No longer what it was, however, and not many of the exhibits are genuine.

MUSÉE NAPOLÉONIEN
In the Town Hall on the Place Foch.
Paintings, busts, pictures and documents,
birth certificate and death-mask.

A BANDERA
Museum of Corsican military history. Rue
Général Levie.

CAPITELLU
History of the town and its population.
Boulevard Danielle Casanova.

Albertacce

MUSÉE ARCHEOLOGIQUE
History of the Niolu from prehistoric times
to the present. Open only in summer.

Aléria

MUSÉE JÉROME CARCOPINO
In the Fort de Matra. Prehistoric archaeological finds and also Greek, Roman, Et-
uscan and Carthaginian exhibits. The
excavation site is open to the public.

Bastia

MUSÉE D'ETHNOGRAPHIE CORSE
Inside the former governor's palace, in
the Citadel. Documentation of everyday,
traditional life. Reminders of the fight for
freedom under Paoli. Collection of amphorae. In the courtyard, the conning-
tower of the submarine Casabianca.

Cervione

MUSEU ETNUGRAFICU
Local history museum for the Castagniccia and the Casinca regions. Behind the
church, in the town hall.

Filitosa

STATION PRÉHISTORIQUE/
CENTRE DE DOCUMENTATION
Menhir statues and archaeological finds.

Ile Rousse

MUSÉE DE LA MER
Marine aquarium located at the end of
the promenade. Peak season only.

Levie

MUSÉE DE LA PRÉHISTOIRE
Housed in the Town Hall. Archaeological finds from the primeval fortresses at Cucuruzzu and Capula. The exhibits are fully
documented.

Luri

MUSÉE DE SENEQUE
Collection of medieval ceramics.

Macinaggio

DÉPOT ARCHEOLOGIQUE
Roman finds from excavations at Mont
Bughju. Information from the Capitainerie
du Port.

Merusaglia

MAISON NATALE DE PASCAL PAOLI
Birthplace of the 'Father of the Father-
land' in the Castagniccia. Mainly memo-
rabilia. His tomb is located in the house
chapel.

Sartène

CENTRE DE LA PRÉHISTOIRE
Menhirs, weapons, utensils and ceramics
from the various archaeological sites in
the region.

LANGUAGE

The official language on the island is
French, usually spoken in the Southern-
French dialect (which is to say that most
final consonants are pronounced). Corsicans also speak their own native tongue,
both a spoken and written language in
its own right and referred to as a lingua
nustrale. This is a blend of Latin with
some Italian and a little bit of French
thrown in. In addition to these identifiable
linguistic elements there are a number of
other ancient, scarcely traceable sources,
such as Iberian. English is spoken by relatively few people on the island, mostly
those engaged in the tourist trade

SPORT

Beach Life

Only a handful of frequently visited beaches
close to the major centres of population
maintain duty lifeguards. In bays that are
enclosed by rocks dangerous currents can
occur on windy days and these can easily
pull swimmers out to sea. Offshore wind
is less frequent, but it still poses risks for
inexperienced surfers as well as for bathers
floating on lilos.

Surfboards and catamarans can usually

Fun on the beach

e hired in beach bars, and on the bus-er east coast you will find *pedalos* (pedal-boats) and even gondolas for hire. Here and there you can also hire extremely noisy water-scooters.

Nude sunbathing is officially only al-owed in certain club-villages, but is qui-tly tolerated if undertaken at the far end of some beaches.

Children

Corsica is a great place to take children on holiday. They are welcomed everywhere and the water at most of the island's sandy beaches is quite shallow and the breakers fairly small. However, if you are taking children it's best to avoid the beaches along the rugged part of the west coast, where the water becomes deep quite suddenly and the undertow can be dangerous.

Golf

There are golf courses at Lucciana, near Bastia; at Punta di Spanu, near Lu-nio/Sant'Ambroggio; and in the Regino Valley near Monticello (both in Balagne); on the road to Bonifacio near Porto-Vec-chio; and at Sperone, near Bonifacio. The latter is the only 18-hole-course, though the other clubs are planning to expand.

Riding

Horse and pony rides, charged by the hour, are available from various rental outlets near the coast. More rewarding, however, are day trips in the company of a guide along the old mule paths in the moun-tains. Here and there you can also hire donkeys or mules.

Angling

Sea-fishing on the beach is mostly unre-stricted, apart from the odd stretch of coastline, but if you fish from a boat the local restrictions do apply. For the rivers and mountain streams you need to have a permit which is then valid for the en-tire island. Information is available from tourist offices, angling clubs, or the near-est town hall.

Diving

Snorkelling is rewarding wherever the wa-ter is clear, with a good mix of light sand and rocks beneath the surface. Diving proper tends mostly to occur on the rocky south and west coasts. Snorkellers can also try their luck at harpooning; anyone ven-turing out with oxygen tanks, though, won't even be allowed to keep a harpoon in the boat. Diving clubs are located at a number of centres around the island.

Hiking

The GR 20 hiking trail runs along the alpine chain between Calenzana on the west coast and Conca, near Porto-Vecchio. It is a challenging undertaking and you should give yourself a good two weeks to cover the full distance of 175km (108 miles). There are only two places along the entire route where you can replenish your provisions, and the mountain huts contain no supplies. Because of this, it is important to make sure you're carrying enough water, particularly in the heat of the summer.

For less experienced hikers and families with relatively grown-up children, the Parc Regional has created the trail known as *Tra Mare e Monti* ('Across Sea and Mountain'), which runs from Calenzana to Cargèse, and there's also another one called *Da Mare a Mare* ('From Sea to Sea') which crosses the island from west to east. At the end of each day along these routes there's usually accommodation with a good meal, or at least the opportunity to shop. There are also local hiking routes, but it's worth remembering that these are only clearly marked within the borders of the Parc Naturel.

USEFUL ADDRESSES

Tourist Information

Information regarding Corsica can be obtained at the French tourist information offices located outside France, at the Agence du Tourisme de la Corse in Ajaccio and at the various local tourist information centres situated throughout the island itself.

Corsica

Agence du Tourisme de la Corse
17, Boulevard du Roi Jérôme, F20000 Ajaccio. Tel: 0495 517777.
Offices de Tourisme are located in the following:
Ajaccio: Place du Marché, from early 1999 Ajaccio. Tel: 0495 515303
Bastia: Place St-Nicolas, 20200 Bastia. Tel: 0495 559696.
Bonifacio: Rue des Deux-Moulins, 20169 Bonifacio. Tel: 0495 731188.
Calvi: Port de Plaisance, 20260 Calvi. Tel: 0495 651667.
Saint-Florent: B.P. 29, 20217 Saint-Florent. Tel: 0495 370604.
In addition to the aforementioned offices there are also tourist information centre (Syndicat d'Initiative) located at the mos popular tourist centres.

France

Air France, 119 Champs Elysées, 7538 Paris, Cedex. Tel: (l) 43 23 81 81; cen tral reservation: (0) 802 802 802.
Nouvelles Frontières, central reservations 0 803 333 333.
Maison de la France, 20 Avenue d l'Opéra, 75001 Paris (no visitors), Tel 0142 967000.

UK and Ireland

Air France, 10 Warwick Street – 1st Floo London W1R 5RA, reservations: 0181 742 6600. Dublin Airport, reservation 01 844 5633.
Consulat Général de France, Colleg House, 29/31 Wrights Lane, London W8 5SH. Tel: 0171-937 1202.
French Government Tourist Office, 178 Piccadilly, London W1V 9DB. Tel: 0171 491 7622.

US and Canada

Air France, New York, 120 West 56th Street; Los Angeles, 725 South Figueroa Street, Suite 3251. Central reservation 800 237 2747.
Montreal, Quebec, 200 Rue Mansfield 15th floor, Montreal H3A 3A3.
Toronto, Ontario, 151 Bloor Street West. Suite 810. Central reservation: 800 667 2747.
Maison de la France/French Government Tourist Office, 610 Fifth Avenue, Suite 222, New York, NY 10020-2452. Tel (212) 757 1125.
9454 Wilshire Boulevard, Beverly Hills, Los Angeles, Ca 90212-2967. Tel: (213) 272 2661.
645 North Michigan Avenue, Suite 630, Chicago, Illinois 60611-2836. Tel: 337 6301 (Business Travel Division: 751 7804).
Cedar Maple Plaza, 2305 Cedar Springs Road, Suite 205, Dallas, Texas 75201. Tel: (214) 720 4010.
1981 McGill College, Tour Esso, Suite 490, Montreal H3A 2W9, Quebec. Tel: (514) 288 4264.
Suite 2405, 1 Dundas Street West, Toronto M5G lZ3 Ontario. Tel: (416) 593 4723.

Embassies and Consulates

American Embassy, 2 Avenue Gabriel, 75382 Paris, Cedex 08. Tel: 0143 122347 (information), 0836 701488 (visas); there is also a consulate in Nice at 31 Rue Maréchal Joffre, 06000 Nice. Tel: 93 88 89 55.

Australian Embassy, 4 Rue Jean-Rey, 75015 Paris. Tel: 0140 593300 (information) 0140 593306 (visas).

British Embassy, 35 Rue du Faubourg-St-Honoré, 75008 Paris. Tel: 0144 513100/01. There is a consulate in Nice at 12 Rue de France, 06000 Nice. Tel: 93 82 32 04.

Canadian Embassy, 35 Avenue Montaigne, 75008 Paris. Tel: 0144 432900.

Irish Embassy, 12 Avenue Foch, 75116 Paris. Tel: 0144 176700

FURTHER READING

Boswell, James. *An Account of Corsica* (contained in 'Boswell on the Grand Tour', Yale Editions, New York and London, 1955). Descriptions of his journey around the island and his visit to Pasquale Paoli.

Carrington, Dorothy. *Granite Island: a Portrait of Corsica* (Penguin paperback, New York and London, 1984).

Chiari, Joseph. *The Scented Isle: a parallel between Corsica and the Scottish Highlands* (Glasgow 1945).

Elliot, Emma Eleanor. *The Life and Letters od Sir Gilbert Elliot* (London 1874). Compiled by the granddaughter of this aristocratic Scot, who as the Viceroy from 1794–96 acquired a love of the island and its inhabitants.

Lear, Edward. *Journal of a Landscape Painter in Corsica* (London 1870). Through both his engravings and his writings, Lear was one of the first to portray the splendours of Corsica to the outside world.

Mérimée, Prosper. *Columba* (Paris 1840). Based on the story of the vendetta that took place in the village of Fozzano in the Sartenais in 1833.

Moracchini-Mazel, Geneviève. *Corse Romane* (Paris 1972). Includes English translation to text describing this illustrated guide to the island's Romanesque churches.

Schütz, Jutta (ed). *Insight Guide: Corsica* (APA, 1999). A comprehensive and richly-illustrated guide to the island and its inhabitants, their history and their heroes.

Thresher, Peter Adam. *Pasquale Paoli: an Enlightened Hero* (London 1970). The most authoritative work on the island's greatest hero.

Vallance, Aylmer. *The Summer King* (London 1956). Absorbing account of the fortunes of Theodor von Neuhof, the German nobleman who wanted to rule Corsica.

Index

ACKNOWLEDGMENTS

Photography	Alphons Schauseil *and*
Page 5T	Leonora Ander
Page 5B	Hartmut Lücke
77	Anita Back
13	Historia Photo
6/7, 16, 28T, 29T, 31T, 32, 36, 37, 38T, 41, 43, 48, 49T, 51, 52T, 52B, 54, 56, 57B, 64, 72, 79, 81, 82T, 83, 86, 89, 91	Neill Menneer
11, 12, 14B, 15, 47	Jutta Schütz
46	Janos Stekovics
27B	Werner Stuhler
Production Editor	Erich Meyer
Handwriting	V.Barl
Cover Design	Klaus Geisler
Cartography	Berndtson & Berndtson

Insight Guides

Alaska
Alsace
Amazon Wildlife
American Southwest
Amsterdam
Argentina
Atlanta
Athens
Australia
Austria
Bahamas
Bali
Baltic States
Bangkok
Barbados
Barcelona
Bay of Naples
Beijing
Belgium
Belize
Berlin
Bermuda
Boston
Brazil
Brittany
Brussels
Budapest
Buenos Aires
Burgundy
Burma (Myanmar)
Cairo
Calcutta
California
Canada
Caribbean
Catalonia
Channel Islands
Chicago
Chile
China
Cologne
Continental Europe
Corsica
Costa Rica
Crete
Crossing America
Cuba
Cyprus
Czech & Slovak
  Republics
Delhi, Jaipur, Agra
Denmark

Dresden
Dublin
Düsseldorf
East African Wildlife
East Asia
Eastern Europe
Ecuador
Edinburgh
Egypt
Finland
Florence
Florida
France
Frankfurt
French Riviera
Gambia & Senegal
Germany
Glasgow
Gran Canaria
Great Barrier Reef
Great Britain
Greece
Greek Islands
Hamburg
Hawaii
Hong Kong
Hungary
Iceland
India
India's Western
  Himalaya
Indian Wildlife
Indonesia
Ireland
Israel
Istanbul
Italy
Jamaica
Japan
Java
Jerusalem
Jordan
Kathmandu
Kenya
Korea
Lisbon
Loire Valley
London
Los Angeles
Madeira
Madrid
Malaysia
Mallorca & Ibiza
Malta

Marine Life in the
  South China Sea
Melbourne
Mexico
Mexico City
Miami
Montreal
Morocco
Moscow
Munich
Namibia
Native America
Nepal
Netherlands
New England
New Orleans
New York City
New York State
New Zealand
Nile
Normandy
Northern California
Northern Spain
Norway
Oman & the UAE
Oxford
Old South
Pacific Northwest
Pakistan
Paris
Peru
Philadelphia
Philippines
Poland
Portugal
Prague
Provence
Puerto Rico
Rajasthan
Rhine
Rio de Janeiro
Rockies
Rome
Russia
St Petersburg
San Francisco
Sardinia
Scotland
Seattle
Sicily
Singapore
South Africa
South America
South Asia

South India
South Tyrol
Southeast Asia
Southeast Asia Wildli
Southern California
Southern Spain
Spain
Sri Lanka
Sweden
Switzerland
Sydney
Taiwan
Tenerife
Texas
Thailand
Tokyo
Trinidad & Tobago
Tunisia
Turkey
Turkish Coast
Tuscany
Umbria
US National Parks Eas
US National Parks We
Vancouver
Venezuela
Venice
Vienna
Vietnam
Wales
Washington DC
Waterways of Europe
Wild West
Yemen

Insight Pocket Guides

Aegean Islands ★
Algarve ★
Alsace
Amsterdam ★
Athens ★
Atlanta ★
Bahamas ★
Baja Peninsula ★
Bali ★
Bali *Bird Walks*
Bangkok ★
Barbados ★
Barcelona ★
Bavaria ★
Beijing ★
Berlin ★
Bermuda ★

nsight Guides

er every major destination in every continent.

Bhutan★
Boston★
British Columbia★
Brittany★
Brussels★
Budapest &
 Surroundings★
Canton★
Chiang Mai★
Chicago★
Corsica★
Costa Blanca★
Costa Brava★
Costa del
 Sol/Marbella★
Costa Rica★
Crete★
Denmark★
Fiji★
Florence★
Florida★
Florida Keys★
French Riviera★
Gran Canaria★
Hawaii★
Hong Kong★
Hungary
Ibiza★
Ireland★
Ireland's Southwest★
Israel★
Istanbul★
Jakarta★
Jamaica★
Kathmandu *Bikes &*
 Hikes★
Kenya★
Kuala Lumpur★
Lisbon★
Loire Valley★
London★
Macau
Madrid★
Malacca
Maldives
Mallorca★
Malta★
Mexico City★
Miami★
Milan★
Montreal★
Morocco★
Moscow
Munich★

Nepal★
New Delhi
New Orleans★
New York City★
New Zealand★
Northern California★
Oslo/Bergen★
Paris★
Penang★
Phuket★
Prague★
Provence★
Puerto Rico★
Quebec★
Rhodes★
Rome★
Sabah★
St Petersburg★
San Francisco★
Sardinia
Scotland★
Seville★
Seychelles★
Sicily★
Sikkim
Singapore★
Southeast England
Southern California★
Southern Spain★
Sri Lanka★
Sydney★
Tenerife★
Thailand★
Tibet★
Toronto★
Tunisia★
Turkish Coast★
Tuscany★
Venice★
Vienna★
Vietnam★
Yogyakarta
Yucatan Peninsula★

★ = *Insight Pocket*
Guides
with Pull out Maps

Insight Compact Guides

Algarve
Amsterdam
Bahamas
Bali
Bangkok

Barbados
Barcelona
Beijing
Belgium
Berlin
Brittany
Brussels
Budapest
Burgundy
Copenhagen
Costa Brava
Costa Rica
Crete
Cyprus
Czech Republic
Denmark
Dominican Republic
Dublin
Egypt
Finland
Florence
Gran Canaria
Greece
Holland
Hong Kong
Ireland
Israel
Italian Lakes
Italian Riviera
Jamaica
Jerusalem
Lisbon
Madeira
Mallorca
Malta
Milan
Moscow
Munich
Normandy
Norway
Paris
Poland
Portugal
Prague
Provence
Rhodes
Rome
St Petersburg
Salzburg
Singapore
Switzerland
Sydney
Tenerife
Thailand

Turkey
Turkish Coast
Tuscany
UK regional titles:
 Bath & Surroundings
 Cambridge & East
  Anglia
 Cornwall
 Cotswolds
 Devon & Exmoor
 Edinburgh
 Lake District
 London
 New Forest
 North York Moors
 Northumbria
 Oxford
 Peak District
 Scotland
 Scottish Highlands
 Shakespeare Country
 Snowdonia
 South Downs
 York
 Yorkshire Dales
USA regional titles:
 Boston
 Cape Cod
 Chicago
 Florida
 Florida Keys
 Hawaii: Maui
 Hawaii: Oahu
 Las Vegas
 Los Angeles
 Martha's Vineyard &
  Nantucket
 New York
 San Francisco
 Washington D.C.
Venice
Vienna
West of Ireland